REVIVAL AND HOLINESS THEOLOGY IN AMERICA
AN ALETHEA IN HEART REPRODUCTION
IN THE SERIES OF
THE COMPLETE WORKS OF CHARLES G. FINNEY.

Lecture Notes on Theology.
Skeletons of a Course of Theological Lectures.
Lectures on Systematic Theology I & II.
Lectures on Revivals of Religion, The Complete Restored Text.
The Way of Salvation.
Sermons on Gospel Themes.
Sermons on Important Subjects.
Lectures to Professing Christians.
How to Experience the Higher Life.
How to Pray to God.
The Right Way to "Train up a Child."
The Character, Claims and Practical Workings of Freemasonry.
Knowing and Loving God.
The Love of God for a Sinning World.
The Dreadful Results of Sin.
The Complete Sermon Collection (almost 400).
The Memoirs of Charles G. Finney.
Letters on Revival and other Matters.
Treasured Memories of Charles G. Finney by his Associates, Students, and Friends.

HOW TO EXPERIENCE THE HIGHER LIFE.

REPUBLISHED BY THE EDITOR.
RICHARD FRIEDRICH OF ALETHEA IN HEART MINISTRIES,
5262 Belding Rd, Belding MI 48809
http://truthinheart.com
(208) 304-2954

AUGUST 2001.

Finney, Charles, 1792-1875.
How to Experience the Higher Life.
How Finney experienced and taught the doctrines of
The higher life, the baptism of the Holy Spirit, and entire sanctification.

Republication of selections of
Finney's Memiors, The oberlin Evangelist,
And the 1851 edition of Systematic Theology.

1. Finney's Baptism of the Holy Ghost in Boston in the winter of 1843-1844. 2. Sermons on holiness, the higher life, and Baptism of the Holy Ghost. 3. Divine manifestations of Christ to the believer.

ISBN 0-9719805-7-8

Second Alethea In Heart edition published in 2002.
Reproduced from Finney's *Memoirs*, *The Oberlin Evangelist*, and the 1851 London edition of *Finney's Systematic Theology*, without altering anything but format.

Copyright 2001
Richard Max Friedrich
All Rights Reserved

MANUFACTURED IN THE UNITED STATES OF AMERICA.

How to Experience the Higher Life.

By

THE REV. CHARLES G. FINNEY

Author of "Lectures on Revivals."

A book that will not only change the church's view of Finney, but will show how he later found the only Way to really know and experience "all the fullness of God."

BELDING:
REPUBLISHED BY THE EDITOR.
RICHARD FRIEDRICH OF ALETHEA IN HEART MINISTRIES,
5262 Belding Rd
Belding, MI 48809 USA.
(208) 304-2954
TruthInHeart.com

August 2001.

CONTENTS.

	PAGE
Forward by the Editor	5

Introduction.
FINNEY'S HIGHER LIFE EXPERIENCE IN 1843.   7

Chapter I.
ABIDING IN CHRIST AND NOT SINNING.
1 John 3:5, 6. December 22, 1858.   19

Chapter II.
GOD'S COMMANDMENTS NOT GRIEVOUS.
1 John 5:3. June 21, 1854.   27

Chapter III.
PRAYER FOR A PURE HEART.
Psalms lxi. 10. March 14, 1849.   44

Chapter IV.
OPEN THOU MINE EYES!
Psalms 119: 18. July 17, 1844.   60

Chapter V.
COMING TO THE WATERS OF LIFE.
John 7:37. September 2, 1846.   88

Chapter VI.
ON DIVINE MANIFESTATIONS.
John 14:15-17; 21-23. March 18, 1846.   103

Chapter VII.
ON PRAYER FOR THE HOLY SPIRIT.
Luke 11:11-13. May 23, 1855.   120

APPENDIX.
RELATIONS OF CHRIST TO THE BELIEVER.   135

FORWARD BY THE EDITOR.

Most people who have heard something of Finney and his revivals do not realize that he experienced a complete overhaul in his relationship with God in the middle of his ministry. He was converted in 1821 and was used in revivals for the next fifty years perhaps more than any man since the times of the apostle Paul. Yet even though thousands were converted in the early years and displayed the remarkable piety, Finney did not see many converts experience the highest privileges that believers can experience through Jesus Christ. He went to Oberlin in the 1830's and while ministering there with President Asa Mahan they came to see that the experiences of Paul ought to be the experiences of all believers. These men, and many students and associates, began thus to teach on the higher life in ways previously neglected and unknown. The details of this fascinating historical event are found in Finney's *Memoirs* and Mahan's *Out of Darkness Into Light* as well as in his *Autobiography*.[1] Finney came to the *fullness* of this experience in his own life later in 1843 as we will see in the introduction. After this baptism his preaching was fuller and noticeably more heavenly. Unfortunately most people only know of him before this change occurred because of all the books and sermons published before that event. So we are endeavoring to bring to the public hundreds of his sermons and other works after this change took place, with hopes that people may get a better picture of Mr. Finney, in that he taught the fullness of the gospel in the second half of his ministry. The selection of sermons below therefore are after this time and illustrate the change in his doctrine and experience concerning the purification of the entire man, and the higher life. This book is composed of unaltered selections

---

[1] Available through Alethea In Heart Ministries: truthinheart.com

from Finney's *Memoirs*, miscellaneous sermons from *The Oberlin Evangelist*, and his 1851 *Systematic Theology*. It was never organized in this manner until the present; and therefore some minor overlap occurs.

Most people familiar with Finney know that his logical powers and natural talents were of the highest development and were therefore a mighty means for revival in the hands of God. Yet his early sermons are sometimes thought of as too dependent upon such natural abilities. Thus people still shy away from his works and would hardly imagine that after his confessed experience he later progressed spiritually *beyond* what he possessed logically. He never lost the stigma of "logic set on fire" after this, but then the *trail* was not so much memories of a mighty man as that of a divine rushing wind leaving the loving spirit of heavenly dew. He is known for his power with God—he is known for his success with God—and now we will begin to know him in a way that will far surpass—we will know him as one swallowed up in Christ as his All in All.

Richard M. Friedrich
   Editor of *The Works of Charles G. Finney*
     And *The Works of Asa Mahan*.

INTRODUCTION.

FINNEY'S HIGHER LIFE EXPERIENCE IN 1843.

FROM
CHARLES G. FINNEY'S MEMOIRS.
CHAPTER XXVII.
ANOTHER WINTER IN BOSTON.
Fall 1843 to March 1844.

IN the fall of 1843, I was called again to Boston. . . .

During this winter, the Lord gave my own soul a very thorough overhauling, and a fresh baptism of His Spirit. I boarded at the Marlborough hotel, and my room in one corner of the chapel building. I had my study there, and adjoining my study a bedroom. My mind was greatly drawn out in prayer, for a long time; as indeed it always has been, when I have labored in Boston. I have been favored there, uniformly, with a great deal of the Spirit of prayer. But this winter, in particular, my mind was exceedingly exercised on the question of personal holiness; and in respect to the state of the church, their want of power with God, and the weakness of the Orthodox churches in Boston, the weakness of their faith, and their want of power in the midst of such a community. The fact that they were making little or no progress in overcoming the errors of the city, greatly affected my mind.

I gave myself to a great deal of prayer. After my evening services, I would retire as early as I well could; but rose up at four O'clock in the morning, because I could sleep no longer, and immediately went to the study, and engaged in prayer. And so deeply was my mind exercised, and so absorbed in prayer, that I frequently continued from the time I arose at four O'clock, till the gong called to breakfast, at eight O'clock.

My days were spent, so far as I could get time—for I had a great deal of company coming constantly to see me—in searching the Scriptures. I read nothing else, all that winter, but my Bible; and a great deal of it seemed new to me. Again the Lord took me, as it were, from Genesis to Revelation. He led me to see the connection of things—how things predicted in the Old Testament had come out in the New Testament—the promises, threatenings, the prophecies and their fulfillment;—and indeed, the whole Scripture seemed to me all ablaze with light, and not only light, but it seemed as if God's Word was instinct with the very *life* of God.

After praying in this way for weeks and months, one morning while I was engaged in prayer, the thought occurred to me, what if, after all this divine teaching, my will is not carried, and this teaching takes effect only in my sensibility? May it not be that my sensibility is affected, by these revelations from reading the Bible, and that my heart is not really subdued by them? At this point several passages of scripture occurred to me, much as this: "Line must be upon line, line upon line, precept upon precept, precept upon precept, here a little, and there a little, that they might go and fall backward, and be snared and taken." The thought that I might be deceiving myself by the states of my sensibility, when it first occurred to me, stung me almost like an adder. It created a pang that I cannot describe. The passages of Scripture that occurred to me, in that direction, for a few moments greatly increased my distress. But directly I was enabled to fall back upon the perfect will of God. I said to the Lord, that if He saw it was wise and best, and that His honor demanded that I should be left to be deluded, and go down to hell, I accepted His will, and I said to Him, "Do with me as seemeth Thee good."

Just before this occurrence, I had had a great struggle to consecrate myself to God, in a higher sense[2] than I had ever

---

[2] Bold text in this chapter added for specific reference to the higher life

before seen to be my duty, or conceived as possible. I had often before, laid my family all upon the altar of God, and left them to be disposed of at His discretion. But at this time that I now speak of, and previously to my finally accepting the will of God, I had had a great struggle about giving up my wife to the will of God. She was in very feeble health, and it was very evident that she could not live long. I about that time had a dream about my wife that had opened the way for the struggle of which I speak. After that dream I attempted to lay her upon the altar, as I had often before done. But I had never before seen so clearly, what was implied in laying her, and all that I possessed, upon the altar of God; and for hours I struggled upon my knees, to give her up unqualifiedly to the will of God. But I found myself unable to do it. I was so shocked and surprised at this, that I perspired profusely with agony. I struggled and prayed until I was exhausted, and found myself entirely unable to give her altogether up to God's will, in such a way as to make no objection to His disposing of her just as He pleased.

This troubled me much. I wrote to my wife, telling her what a struggle I had had, and the concern that I had felt at not being willing to commit her unqualifiedly to the perfect will of God. This was but a very short time before I had this temptation, as it now seems to me to have been, of which I have spoken, when those passages of Scripture came up distressingly to my mind, and when the bitterness, almost of death seemed, for a few moments, to possess me, at the thought that my religion might be of the Sensibility only, and that God's teaching might have taken effect only in my feeling. But as I said, I was enabled, after struggling for a few moments with this discouragement and bitterness, which I have since attributed to a fiery dart of Satan, to fall back, in a deeper sense than I had ever done before upon the infinitely blessed and perfect will of God. I then told the Lord that I

---

experience.

had such confidence in Him, that I felt perfectly willing, to give myself, my wife and my family, and all to be disposed of without qualification according to His own views and will. That if He thought it best and wise to send me to hell, to do so, and I would consent to it. As to my wife, I felt also entirely willing to lay her, body and soul, upon the altar, without the least misgiving in my mind in delivering her up to the perfect will of God.

I then had a deeper view of what was implied in consecration to God, than I ever had before. I spent a long time upon my knees, in considering the matter all over, and giving up everything to the will of God; the interests of the church, the progress of religion, the conversion of the world, and the salvation or damnation of my own soul, as the will of God might decide. Indeed I recollect, that I went so far as to say to the Lord, with all my heart, that He might do anything with me or mine, to which His blessed will could consent. That I had such perfect confidence in His goodness and love, as to believe that He could consent to do nothing, to which I could object. I felt a kind of holy boldness, in telling Him to do with me just as seemed to Him good. That He could not do anything that was not perfectly wise and good; and therefore I had the best of grounds for accepting whatever He could consent to in respect to me and mine. So deep and perfect a resting in the will of God I had never before known.

What has appeared strange to me is this, that I could not get hold of my former hope; nor could I recollect with any freshness any of the former seasons of communion and divine assurance that I had experienced. I may say that I gave up my hope, and rested everything upon a new foundation. I mean I gave up my hope from any past experience, and recollect telling the Lord, that I did not know whether He intended to save me or not. Nor did I feel concerned to know. I was willing to abide the event. I said that if I found that He kept me, and worked in me by His Spirit, and was preparing me for heaven, working holiness and eternal life in my soul, I should take it for granted that He intended to save me; that if, on the other hand, I found myself empty of divine strength and light and love, I should conclude that He saw it wise and expedient to send me to hell; and that in either event I would accept His will. My mind settled into a perfect stillness.

This was early in the morning; and through the whole of that day, I seemed to be in a state of perfect rest, body and soul. The question frequently arose in my mind, during the day, "Do you still adhere to your consecration, and abide in the will of God?" I said without hesitation, "Yes, I take nothing back. I have no reason for taking anything back; I went no farther in pledges and professions than was reasonable. I have no reason for taking anything back;—I do not *want* to take anything back." The thought that I might be lost did not distress me. Indeed, think as I might during that whole day, I could not find in my mind the least fear, the least disturbing emotion. Nothing troubled me. I was neither elated nor depressed; I was neither, as I could see, joyful or sorrowful. My confidence in God was perfect, my acceptance of His will was perfect, and my mind was as calm as heaven.

Just at evening, the question arose in my mind, "What if God should send me to hell,—what then?" "Why, I would not object to it." "But *can* He send a person to hell," was the next inquiry, "who accepts His will in the sense in which you do?" This inquiry was no sooner raised in my mind than settled. I said, "No, it is impossible. Hell could be no hell to me, if I accepted God's perfect will." This sprung a vein of joy in my mind, that kept developing more and more, for weeks and months, and indeed I may say, for years. For years my mind was too full of joy to feel much exercised with anxiety on any subject. My prayer that had been so fervent, and protracted during so long a period, seemed all to run out into, "Thy will be done." It seemed as if my desires were all met. What I had been praying for for myself, I had received in a way that I least expected. Holiness to the Lord seemed to be inscribed on all the exercises of my mind. I had such strong faith that God would accomplish all His perfect will, that I could not be *careful* about *anything*. The great anxieties about which my mind had been exercised, during my seasons of agonizing prayer, seemed to be set aside; so that for a long time, when I went to God, to commune with Him—as I did very, very frequently—I would fall on my knees, and find it impossible to ask for anything, with any earnestness except that His will might be done in earth as it was done in heaven. My prayers were swallowed up in that; and I often found myself smiling, as it were, in the face of God, and saying that I did not want anything. I was very sure that He would accomplish all His wise and good pleasure; and with that my soul was entirely satisfied.

Here I lost that great struggle in which I had been engaged for so long a time, and began to preach to the congregation in accordance with this my new and enlarged experience. There was a considerable number in the church, and that attended my preaching, who understood me; and they saw from my preaching what had been, and what was, passing in my mind. I presume the people were more sensible than I was myself, of the great change in my manner of preaching. Of course, my mind was too full of the subject to preach anything except a full and present salvation in the Lord Jesus Christ.

At this time it seemed as if my soul was wedded to Christ, in a sense in which I had never had any thought or conception of before. The language of the Song of Solomon, was as natural to me as my breath. I thought I could understand well the state of mind he was in when he wrote that song; and concluded then, as I have ever thought since, that that song was written by him, after he had been reclaimed from his great backsliding. I not only had all the freshness of my first love, but a vast accession to it. Indeed the Lord lifted me so much above anything that I had experienced before, and taught me so much of the meaning of the Bible, of Christ's relations and power and willingness, that I often found myself saying to Him, "I had not known or conceived that any such thing was true." I then realized what is meant by the saying, "that he is able to do *exceeding abundantly* above all that we ask or think." He did at that time teach me, indefinitely above all that I had ever asked or thought. I had had no conception of the length and breadth, and height and depth, and efficiency of his grace. It seemed then to me that that passage, "My grace is sufficient for thee," meant so much, that it was wonderful I had never understood it before. I found myself exclaiming, "Wonderful!" "Wonderful!" "Wonderful!" as these revelations were made to me. I could understand then what was meant by the prophet when he said, "His name shall be called Wonderful, Counselor, the mighty God, the everlasting Father, the Prince of peace."

I spent nearly all the remaining part of the winter, till I was obliged to return home, in instructing the people in regard to the fullness there was in Christ. But I found that I preached over the heads of the masses of the people. They did not understand me. There was, indeed, a goodly number that did; and they were wonderfully blessed in their souls, and made more progress in the divine life, as I have reason to believe, than in all their lives before. But the little church that was formed there was not composed of materials that could, to any considerable extent, work healthfully and efficiently together. The outside opposition to them was great. The mass even of professors of religion in the city, did not sympathize with them at all. The people of the churches generally were in no state to receive my views of sanctification; and although there were *individuals* in nearly all the churches, who were deeply interested and greatly blessed, yet as a general thing the testimony that I bore was unintelligible to them.

Some of them could see where I was. One evening I recollect that Deacon Proctor and Deacon Safford, after hearing my preaching, and seeing the effect upon the congregation, came up to me after I came out of the pulpit and said, "Why, you are a great way ahead of us in this city, and a great way ahead of our ministers. How can we get our ministers to come and hear these truths?" I replied, "I do not know. But I wish they could see things as I do; for it does seem to me infinitely important that there should be a higher standard of holiness in Boston." They said it was; and seemed exceedingly anxious to have those truths laid before the people in general. They were good men, as the Boston people well know; but what pains they really took, to get their ministers and people to attend, I cannot say.

I labored that winter mostly for a revival of religion among Christians. The Lord prepared me to do so by the great work He wrought in my own soul. Although I had much of the divine life working within me; yet, as I said, so far did what I experienced that winter exceed all that I had before experienced, that at times I could not realize that I had ever before been truly in communion with God.

To be sure I *had* been, often and for a long time; and this I knew when I reflected upon it, and remembered through what I had so often passed. It appeared to me, that winter as if it is probably when we get to heaven, our views and joys, and holy exercises, will so far surpass anything that we have ever experienced in this life, that we shall be hardly able to recognize the fact that we had any religion, while in this world. I had in fact oftentimes experienced inexpressible joys, and very deep communion with God; but all this had fallen so into the shade, under my enlarged experience that winter, that frequently I would tell the Lord that I had never before had any conception of the wonderful things revealed in His blessed Gospel, and the wonderful grace there is in Christ Jesus. This language, I knew when I reflected upon it, was *comparative*; but still all my former experiences, for the time, seemed to be sealed up, and almost lost sight of.

As the great excitement of that season subsided, my mind became more calm. I saw more clearly the different steps of my Christian experience, and came to recognize the connection of things, as all wrought by God from beginning to end. But since then I have never had those great struggles, and long protracted seasons of agonizing prayer before I could get hold of full rest in God, that I had often experienced. Since then it is quite another thing to prevail with God in my own experience, from what it was before. I can come to God with more calmness, because with more perfect confidence. He enables me now to *rest* in Him, and let everything sink into His perfect will, with much more readiness than ever before the experience of that winter.

I have felt since then a religious freedom, a religious buoyancy and delight in God and in His Word, a steadiness of faith, a Christian liberty and overflowing love, that I had only experienced, I may say, *occasionally* before that. I do not mean that such exercises had been rare to me before; for they had been frequent and often repeated, but never *abiding* as they have been since. My bondage seemed to be at that time entirely broken; and since then I have had the freedom of a child with a loving parent. It seems to me that I can find God *within* me in such a sense that I can rest upon Him and be quiet, lay my heart in his Hand, and nestle down in His perfect will and have no carefulness or anxiety.

I speak of these exercises as *habitual* since that period; but I cannot affirm that they have been altogether unbroken, for in 1860, during a fit of sickness, I had a season of great depression and wonderful humiliation. But the Lord brought me out of it, into an established peace and rest.

A few years after this season of refreshing in Boston of which I speak, that beloved wife of whom I have spoken, died.

This was to me a great affliction. However I did not feel any murmuring, or the least resistance to the will of God. I gave her up to God, without any resistance whatever, that I can recollect. But it was to me a great sorrow. The night after she died, I was lying in my lonely bed, and some Christian friends were sitting up in the parlor and watching out the night. I had been asleep for a little while and awoke, and the thought of my bereavement flashed over my mind with such power! My wife was gone! I should never hear her speak again, nor see her face! Her children were motherless! What should I do? My brain seemed to reel, as if my mind would swing from its pivot. I rose instantly from my bed exclaiming, "I shall be deranged if I cannot rest in God!" The Lord soon calmed my mind for that night; but still at times seasons of sorrow would come over me that were almost overwhelming.

One day I was upon my knees communing with God upon the subject, and all at once he seemed to say to me, "You loved your wife?" "Yes," I said. "Well, did you love her for her own sake, or for your sake? Did you love her, or yourself? If you loved her for her own sake, why do you sorrow that she is with Me? Should not her happiness with Me, make you rejoice instead of mourn, if you loved her for her own sake?" "Did you love her," He seemed to say to me, "for *my* sake? If you loved her for my sake, surely you would not grieve that she is with me. Why do you think of *your loss*, and lay so much stress upon that, instead of thinking of *her gain*? Can you be sorrowful when she is so joyful and happy? If you loved her for her own sake, would you not rejoice in her joy, and be happy in her happiness?"

I can never describe the feelings that came over me when I seemed to be thus addressed. It produced an instantaneous change in the whole state of my mind in regard to the loss of my wife. From that moment sorrow on account the event was gone forever. I no longer thought of her as dead, but as alive and in the midst of the glories of heaven. My faith was at this time so strong and my mind so enlightened, that it seemed as if I could enter into the very state of mind in which she was in heaven; and if there is any such thing as communing with an absent spirit, or with one who is in heaven, I seemed to commune with her. Not that I ever supposed she was present in such a sense that I at that time communed personally with her. But it seemed as if I knew what her state of mind was there, what profound, unbroken rest, in the perfect will of God. I could see that was heaven, and I experienced it in my own soul. And I have never to this day got over of these views. They frequently recur to me,—as the very state of mind in which the inhabitants of heaven are, and I can see why they are in such a state of mind.

My wife had died in a heavenly frame of mind. Her rest in God was so perfect that it seemed to me that after she was dead she only entered into a fuller apprehension of the love and faithfulness of God, so as to confirm and perfect forever her trust in God and her union with His will. These are experiences in which I have lived a great deal since that time. But in preaching I have found that nowhere can I preach those truths on which my own soul delights to live, and be understood, except it be by a very small number. Much as that subject has been dwelt upon here, I have never found that more than a very few, even of our own people, appreciate and receive those views of God and Christ, and the fullness of His present salvation, upon which my own soul still delights to feed. Everywhere I am obliged to come down to where the people are, in order to make them understand me; and in every place where I have preached for many years, I have found the churches in so low a state as to be utterly incapable of apprehending and appreciating what I regard as the most precious truths of the whole Gospel.

When preaching to impenitent sinners I am obliged, of course, to go back to first principles. In my own experience I have so long passed these outposts and first principles, that I cannot live upon those truths. I however have to preach them to the impenitent to secure their conversion. When I preach the Gospel, I can preach the atonement, conversion, and many of the prominent views of the Gospel that are appreciated and accepted by those who are young in the religious life; and by those also who have been long in the church of God, and have made very little advancement in the knowledge of Christ. But it is only now and then that I find it really profitable to the people of God to pour out to them the fullness that my own soul sees in Christ. In this place there is a larger number of persons by far that understand me and devour that class of truths, than in any other place that I ever saw; but even here the majority of professors of religion do not understandingly embrace those truths. They do not object, they do not oppose; and so far as they understand, they are convinced. But as a matter of experience they are ignorant of the power of the highest and most precious truths of the Gospel of salvation, in Christ Jesus.

. . . .

This was not my last winter by any means in Boston. I have much more to say, in another place, of revivals there. As to the number of conversions in that city that winter, I cannot speak other than to say that they must have been upon the whole numerous, as I was visited in my room almost constantly from day to day by inquirers from different parts of the city. However, as I have said, I think the greater number of inquirers that winter were professors of religion, whose minds were stirred up mightily to inquire after a higher Christian life.

Chapter I.

ABIDING IN CHRIST AND NOT SINNING.

Reported by Rev. Henry Cowles. December 22, 1858.

"And ye know that he was manifested to take away our sins, and in him is no sin. Whosoever abideth in him sinneth not; whosoever sinneth hath not seen him, neither known him."

—1 John 3:5, 6

The course of thought in this passage is exceedingly significant. First, John affirms one of the plainest truths in the whole gospel system, viz. that Jesus Christ came in human flesh *to take away our sins*. "Thou shalt call his name Jesus, for he shall save his people from their sins."[3] This first truth of the gospel he might well introduce with the words— "Ye know"—for no Christian could be supposed to be ignorant of this.

He next advances to another fact in the gospel system— "In him, Christ, was no sin." He must needs be himself sinless—else he could not be adapted to save his people from their sins. His example must shine in the glory of a sinless purity; he must have no sin of his own to de-bar him from communion with the Father.

The next step in the chain of thought is that whosoever abideth in the sinless One cannot be sinning himself. To come into relations so close, so intimate, with Jesus Christ is utterly incompatible with present actual sinning. He that is now sinning knows not Christ as his Savior—"hath not seen him neither known him." Precisely this is what John affirms.

He who abides in Christ is not sinning; he doth not commit sin. This is plainly declared.

---

[3] Matthew 1:21.

Hence it becomes of the utmost consequence, first, to understand what it is to *be in Christ*. On this point our notions should be, not loose and vague, but clear and definite. It must be, to the real Christian life, a matter of untold importance.

1. Being in Christ implies that we are *out of* ourselves, in the sense in which selfish men are in themselves. It implies that we renounce ourselves as to any will or way of our own. A selfish heart regards itself and its own interests as supreme. The selfish man lives to himself. Self is the precise end for which he lives, labors, plans and cares. Hence, concisely speaking, he is *in himself*. But to be in Christ, he must cease to live and to be in himself, and must in the same sense, come to be and to live, in Christ.

2. Being in Christ implies that we commit ourselves to him, to be pardoned by his blood, quickened by his grace, controlled by his will. I often think we are so much in the habit of using these terms—"commit ourself to Christ;" "consecrate ourself to him"—that we come to miss the sense; perhaps we learn to slip over it without getting a full impression, and it may be, without any just impression of the rich and intense meaning. Who that has once felt its full significance does not see that it amounts to far more than that loose notion that so often goes with the phrase?

To commit yourself to Christ, implies that you merge yourself in him—make him your end of life—make his glory your supreme end in all you do. You merge your will in his will, so that, apart from his, you have no will of your own. You *wish* for nothing, save what pleases him.

In some human relations, we have an approximation to this. One so merges himself in the will of another as to think nothing of his own will. The subordinate officer so merges his own will in the will of his commander that he seeks only to learn and to carry out *his* will. In times of peril, where safety depends on the energetic action of one leading mind—that, say of a sea-captain in a storm, his men think of nothing but to hang upon his will, catch its intimations and hasten to obey.

Of course these are only faint illustrations, for we must sink into Christ in a far higher sense than we ever should, or safely can, into any other being.

Again, it implies that we take *refuge in Him*. In many beautiful passages of Scripture, the Christian is represented as taking refuge in Jesus Christ. He is a great rock which casts its grateful shadow in a very desert land; or a jutting rock, cleft on the mountain side, under which one may find shelter from the storm; or a strong tower into which the righteous runs and is safe. So faith takes refuge in him from all the evils of this evil world, and from the more dire wrath that is to come! Faith seeks refuge in him as an atoning sacrifice—as one who has laid his life down for the sins of the world; also as a righteous Advocate before God who always prevails and who will surely plead our cause.

So the believer, by faith, loses himself in Christ. He no longer appears as one making atonement for his past sins; he thinks of no such thing, nor does he appear as his own advocate before God; he dares not—would not; it is enough for him that he has Jesus Christ.

In some respects the wife loses herself in her husband. According to the law of some countries, she is no longer known in law; she relinquishes her name, her property under certain contingencies, and is known only as being in him. True, some of these laws may have gone too far and may have become odious and offensive; yet as an illustration of the point in hand, they are none the less pertinent. None need fear that they shall be too entirely lost in Christ. To be lost in him is man's highest peace and glory.

Again, this relation to Christ accepts him as our "Paracletus," in the sense of 1 John 2:1—"If any man sin, we have a Paracletos with the Father, Jesus Christ, the righteous." This significant term denotes a next friend, a legal advocate who pleads your cause and who appears *for us* before the courts. This is a most beautiful figure. Christ takes his people into himself; hides them in himself so that he appears for them and they are not seen. How expressive!

Again, by Scripture figure, we are in him as members of his body. He is the Head—the great center and fountain of nervous energy; from which the vital currents flow out to every member of the body. Thus to be in Christ is to be constantly supplied with life-power from him, our Head.

It implies, of course, that we are fully possessed and controlled by his presence. The old *self* is dead and Christ becomes our life. This is one of the most common figures used in Scripture.

Now to those who have never passed through the outer courts into the inner sanctuary of the great spiritual temple, this may seem all dark. Some seem to suppose that the ancient temple did not prefigure our earthly relationships to Christ, but only the heavenly, and therefore they do not once dream that they are permitted now to enter into the holy of Holies. They content themselves to live as the ancient Jews did—drawing never any nearer than the outer court and never assuming it possible for them while they live on earth to have free access within the vail to the very presence-chamber of Jehovah. They forget that the vail of that temple has been rent in twain, and that the fullest possible access is offered now to all Christ's people

"He that abideth thus in him *sinneth not*."

I understand this to be true in the sense that his disposition to sin is taken away, and his mind is drawn into the opposite attitude—that of true love to God and obedience. He no longer has a selfish disposition; the moral attitude of his soul is reversed.

Again, it is true in the sense that, abiding in Christ, we live a life of faith. The heart depends on Christ for its strength, moment by moment, as little children live a life of faith on their parents, while they are drawn by love and live in constant trust. See when the father enters the room, the little ones run to meet him for a smile and a caress. They expect their daily bread from his hands. More yet, their hungry souls live on the tokens of his love and approbation. This is faith working by love. So the Christian lives not in himself, but in Christ. There is no life to him, out of Christ. The fact is, there is a wonderful difference between living on one's self and living on Christ. He who lives on himself is forever anxious, restive, as one who is conscious of being too weak to bear his own burdens; but he who lives on Christ is out of weakness made strong with a strength all above his own. He knows what it is to repose on Christ.

One cannot live in sin while he abides in Christ, because *so to abide implies a life of love.*

This inexpressibly near and precious relation to Christ, called "abiding in him," must surely include love to him as the ruling element. You are in Christ as friend is one with friend. Thus in him, you honor his name, love his character, devote yourself to his interests. To do this is to be controlled by love.

The spirit of love goes to keeping Christ's commandments. Our Lord said—"He that hath my commandments and keepeth them, he it is that loveth me,"—implying that obedience is the natural and necessary outgrowth of love. It should be always understood that love is the underlying principle of all obedience—nothing is obedience but that which springs from love. On the other hand, we cannot disobey so long as love rules the heart.

To be in Christ, therefore, is a state of mind which by its own nature excludes sin. Some strangely suppose that they are in Christ as a sort of Federal Head—a representative, in this governmental sense. In this way, they suppose themselves to have an "imputed righteousness"—and to have this, whether they have any personal righteousness or not. I fear they will not be likely to have any other, unless they come to know him in a more intimate and heart-affecting relation. True, there is a sense in which we are *in Christ* as our Head—as has been already indicated in our reference to the Bible figure which makes him the head and his people members of his body.

It must not be forgotten that all sin is voluntary disobedience and cannot be anything else. To make anything else sin, is to talk nonsense. Living in Christ, therefore, must exclude sinning.

It is generally admitted that this text means so much as this—Those who abide in Christ do not sin *habitually*;—although there are some who would not say this, for they hold that one may be in Christ and yet live a long time in constant sinning. But in my view this text must mean more than that men do not *sin habitually*. If John had meant only this, why did he not say this?

Besides, abiding in Christ must be more than this, else it does not meet our wants. We need something better and more than being kept from sinning habitually. We need something that will save us really *from sinning*. Nothing less can supply the great want of our fallen life.

In the case of one who truly abides in Christ in the exercise of a living, active faith, to sin—to disobey God— involves a contradiction in terms. To say that one sins while in the exercise of faith and of love, is absurd. Thus the Bible testifies:—"If any man be *in Christ*, he is a new creature" —not merely *ought* to be, but is. So throughout the Bible. I know not one passage, descriptive of being in Christ, which does not imply living without sin. If it were otherwise—if faith in Christ for salvation from sin left the soul yet in sin, then is faith in Christ a failure; for being in Christ by faith has for its special object, victory over sin. And faith is declared to be that which gives the victory over the world. (1 John 5:4)

Hence when we sin, we are no longer in Christ, but out of Christ. This is implied in the text, and it equally follows from the very nature of being in him.

I am often amazed that people should think they have faith when they have not even so much as conviction of the great truths pertaining to Christ. To be in Christ, men must not only know and feel those truths, but they must receive them to their hearts in love.

Faith holds on upon the sustaining arm of Jesus. Thus holding fast, you are sustained. It is only when you let go that you fall. Then you lose his protection, you fail of his support and lose his power. If while you are in vital union with Christ, you sin, then of course he has failed to keep you. The remedy of God's own providing against sin proves unreliable. Reverting to my own experience some years since, there was a long time in which I could see my difficulty. I thought I had faith, but I could see many things in myself that were all wrong—all selfish. My mind became exceedingly exercised and anxious; I could not live so. I even began to question whether I had not misunderstood the Bible by giving its promises too much meaning. I was anxious lest I had overstrained the promises and thereby had come to expect more than God ever intended to grant. I became greatly straitened in my soul until at length I said before the Lord most solemnly—"If thou hast done all for me that is provided in the gospel for thy people, then I am disappointed. I expected more. The gospel has not saved me from sin."

I cannot say that I clearly saw that I had availed myself of all there is in the gospel, but my mind was dark and doubtful. So far forth as my preaching was to Christians, it fell far short of the fullness of the gospel. But now my own experience agonized me and in great anguish and by no means impudently or reproachfully, but in the agony of my soul, I spread out my sorrows and discouragements before the Lord.

It was then I saw that, instead of expecting too much, I had expected too little. I had not expected enough. I had by no means attached to these promises their rich meaning, their full and glorious sense.

You need to understand, brethren, that you may be in a general covenant relation to Christ, and yet not have this personal faith and this intimate union which saves the soul from sinning, because it so unites us to Christ. The ancient Jews were in this general relation, yet many of them failed of the particular and close union of which our text speaks. Many thousands of them did not receive Christ in a saving sense. Obviously they did not so receive him any farther than they were actually saved.

Do any say—*How shall we get into Christ?* How can we attain to this peculiar and soul-transforming union?

In the first place do not begin with assuming that the thing is exceedingly difficult. Do not impeach your loving Savior by supposing that He is so far off and so averse that you can have at least but a faint hope of ever finding him. No indeed; for lo, HE CALLETH THEE even now; arise and go to him. He seeks this very union.

Then the next and main thing is to cast out from your heart all other lovers—all rivals to your Lord. Let your heart go out to him alone. Let your will be lost in his will; not lost in the sense of being annihilated, but in the better sense of being *submitted*—merged in his will. Let it be enough for you to know and follow his will.

Dismiss all selfish ideas and all selfish pursuits. Cease to form selfish schemes, or to scramble after selfish good. Be satisfied with Christ and his love; so shall he accept your heart's love and make you his own.

Chapter II.

GOD'S COMMANDMENTS NOT GRIEVOUS.

Reported by Rev. Henry Cowles. June 21, 1854.

"His commandments are not grievous." 1st. JOHN 5:3.

The commandments here spoken of are God's. The whole verse reads—"For this is the love of God, that we keep His commandments, and His commandments are not grievous." It is elsewhere said, we may know we love God because we love His children. Here the order is reversed;—"we know we love the children of God when we love God and keep His commandments." Both statements are true. If we truly and rightly love men we shall love God also; and if God, then we shall love His children too.

"Grievous," in our text means oppressive, heavy to be borne; yet not heavy in the physical, but in the moral, sense.

I. And here in the outset we must enquire when a commandment may be said to be grievous, and how we may know whether it is truly so regarded or not. What are those qualities and relations which constitute a commandment really *grievous*? Have we any certain test, any sure means of knowing?

We have. God has given us a moral nature by which we may judge, and by which indeed we cannot but judge. Indeed, God requires us to judge by the decisions of this very nature, a requisition which assumes that His written word imposes no precepts on us inconsistent with the moral nature He has given us. It should not be overlooked that God has given us two volumes of revelation, the one written; the other implanted in our constitution. It is safe therefore to assume that the precepts of the one cannot be in conflict with the unquestionable decisions of the other.

Upon this principle, we know,

(1.) That a commandment, impossible to be fulfilled, must be pronounced grievous. We cannot help pronouncing it so, let who ever will affirm the contrary.

(2.) The same is true of a commandment that is unreasonable, one which our moral sense affirms to be so.

A commandment may be unreasonable in many respects; e.g. if it be manifestly unnecessary; the result of capricious severity. If we say this, we should say, that the command is unreasonable, and therefore grievous.

Supposing we know beyond question that the commandments are unnecessary, then if they require great things under great and solemn penalties, they are a great grievance; if under infinite penalties, then they are infinitely grievous; if under light penalties, then they are a light grievance. If the things required are not important, and yet are enforced by grave and fearful penalties, the commands are clearly grievous. Every sane mind necessarily affirms this to be the case.

(3.) A partial commandment is grievous. If it requires different things of persons under the same circumstances; if it has respect of persons, we condemn it as grievous.

Again, if it were difficult to be obeyed, even by the well disposed, and great penalties were attached to disobedience; if under the best circumstances and with the utmost facilities, obedience were scarcely possible, and failure almost certain, this would be grievous.

Again, if we were required to secure any given end and the requisite means were not within our reach, and are not furnished us by the Power that makes the requisition; if we were required to make brick without straw, or to convert the world without the requisite agencies and powers, and the commands were enforced by heavy penalties, this must be regarded as greatly grievous.

Or, if the command were unadapted to our nature or opposed to our highest and best interests; or if the possibility of obeying it were precluded by our circumstances, or by our relations, and we are laid under the burden of heavy penalties to do these things, this would be truly grievous. We could not possibly regard it otherwise.

We should regard a commandment grievous if it required anything more than honest intention and best endeavor, inasmuch as whatever lies outside of and beyond this must be impossible to us. What we cannot do with the best intention and the utmost endeavor, we cannot do at all. This, therefore, would be grievous.

Or yet again, if the interests to be protected by law were of vast importance, and yet were protected by only a slight penalty, such a law might well be deemed grievous by those who had interests demanding protection. You would regard it as a most grievous law which should propose to protect your life by a penalty of only 37 ½ cents.

Or if a trifling end were set up, but a fearful penalty were attached, this also would be grievous.

II. When a commandment is not grievous.

It is not grievous merely because it conflicts with our unreasonable desires. If the desires are contrary to reason, it is not unreasonable that laws should cross them.

Law is not grievous because opposed to the selfishness of men. A precept may be perfectly, infinitely opposed to selfishness, and yet be far from being grievous.

It is not grievous because of its being opposed to our self-will. A self-will that is arbitrary and capricious is no standard by which to judge of law.

Law is not grievous when it merely opposes what conscience also opposes. If law does not conflict with a good and sound conscience, all is right, for conscience is the reason judging on moral subjects—the faculty constituted of God for this end. If conscience be for it, therefore, it cannot be grievous.

No law is grievous which requires only that which is for our highest good. This, our reason necessarily affirms.

If the *object* of the precept is to secure our own highest good, it cannot be regarded by us as grievous, for its spirit is altogether good.

Now do not say that in these statements I am dogmatizing. I am only affirming self-evident propositions. They need only a clear statement to appear to every mind self-evident.

If the law forbids nothing except what would be injurious to us, it is all right.

If it requires us to deny ourselves for the good of others, all is right, provided this self-denial will be for our own highest good. If it will be greater good to us than the sacrifice is an evil; if the self-denial, though real and great, gives us back more than an equivalent, the law which requires it is by no means grievous. Especially is this true if the self-denial not only gives us a greater good, but is an essential and only means of securing our highest good. By no means can this be deemed grievous, requiring of us a self-denial, of which the more we exercise, the greater good we secure.

A law is not grievous where it requires of us simple honesty—a regard to the rights of others, equal to our regard for our own. This cannot be grievous. This may be honest and right if it requires no more of us than we require of others conscientiously. Who can pronounce such a commandment to be grievous?

I shall proceed by and by to enquire whether God's commandments have these qualities and this character; but at present, I am discussing the subject only in its general and abstract form. So doing, we may perhaps better establish the principles that underlie the subject.

A command cannot be said to be grievous when it requires of us only the reasonable employment of all we have and are.

For so much is reasonable, no matter what the particular service may be under the circumstances. It were a contradiction to say it is unreasonable to require a reasonable service of active powers, made for useful action, or of means of usefulness, put in our hands by our Creator.

That cannot be unreasonable or grievous which simply requires of us a right voluntary state. We know ourselves to have a free will, the power to originate our own volitions. This is a thing of which we are absolutely certain from our consciousness. We do *not* certainly know that we can move our own muscles. The law of connection between the will and the muscles is sometimes suspended. You might find it to be so in any effort you might make. But you know you can control your own will. You may try this at any time; and you will find it so. You also believe and assume it to be so, of everybody else, of sane and sound mind.

Now, therefore, if God's love requires of you only a right state of your will, and those acts and states which follow naturally from a right state of the will, no man can reasonably feel that this is grievous, or can honestly pronounce it to be so.

A commandment is not grievous when it requires nothing capricious, nothing unnecessary, nothing hard to the well-disposed; and threatens disobedience with only the proper penalties.

Again, it cannot be deemed grievous when we could not be satisfied if it required nothing less than it does; when we ourselves, in all honesty, are constrained to say, it is all right; but if anything less were required, or if its requisitions were enforced by a less penalty, we should say—it is wrong. Especially if we are aware that any other course than that indicated in the precept would be hard or even ruinous—hard in the sense in which sin is hard, and ruinous in the sense in which sin is ruinous.

Again, if it requires us to do nothing for which help is not provided—all the help requisite in the case—this is not grievous. If it tenders to us all the appropriate instrumentalities necessary to make us practically obedient, we cannot regard it as grievous.

Nor again, when it is easily understood by the well disposed. If the law were above our reach, as the ancient king nailed his on a pillar too high to read,—you might complain; but since the law is made so plain that he who runs may read it, you cannot regard it as grievous. Especially you cannot so regard it, since the will is taken for the deed, and it is always accepted if there be a willing mind and a good intention. e.g. Suppose the command be to convert the world. You set yourself to do it. You live for this purpose. You honestly intend to do all you can for this end. You fail only because, having exhausted your powers, the work has proved too great for your strength. Very well; you shall have your reward, as if you had succeeded and done all. What! say you, is the will taken for the deed? Yes; when the whole heart is in it and you do your utmost. Ah, said that missionary, as he returned with ruined health and blighted hopes, "I have *failed!* My mission purpose and endeavors have been a *failure!*" Perhaps not. You have been to Africa, and are driven back by the climate. Very well, you have obeyed the command and you shall not fail of your reward.

III. I am next to consider in special the commandments of God, to see whether they can rightly be deemed grievous.

1. Negatively, as to what they are *not* and do *not* require.

Not one of them requires anything above the use of our own powers, and nothing which goes beyond the dictates and approval of our own reason. The precepts of the law and of the gospel are identical in spirit and in general character, neither requiring of us anything more than we can do, nor anything not in harmony with our reason.

God's law does not require us to undo anything we have done that is wrong—in the season of putting it back to its position before being done. This might be, and usually would be, impossible. God only requires us to undo our present wrong purposes and states of mind; the wrong deeds of the past. He has provided a way to forgive; the present wrong of our heart He makes our concern.

He does not require us to make satisfaction for the wrong done, either by atonement, or by making up for the wrong we have done.

He does not require us to save ourselves and secure the salvation of our own souls, without His aid and grace. He neither requires or expects that we shall save anybody else by our own wisdom or efforts. He knows this is naturally impossible.

He does not ask us to work out a legal righteousness for the future. He does not make perfect obedience to law the condition of our salvation. This, if required, would be grievous, inasmuch as we have entirely broken the law and forfeited all hope in that direction.

Nor does He require us to fulfil the law in the future without reference to His grace, and without His aid, presented in the gospel. Nor does He demand that we shall bear our own burdens, overcome our temptations, and fight our spiritual battles—without His grace, guidance and strength. He does not expect us to be our own guide, to find our own way, and to create our own success.

Again, God requires nothing that will in the least mar our own happiness, or interfere with our true interests. Nothing inconsistent with our highest progress in true improvement; nothing that naturally retards our rapid advancement in all that is good.

He does not require us to love Him above our ability.

The law specifies—"Thou shalt love the Lord thy God with all thy heart, with all thy soul, with all thy mind and with all thy strength." With *whose* mind—and *whose* strength? Only thine own. And with how much of this mind and strength?

Only with all. Nothing more. It were simply absurd to say that this is impossible; and therefore it is impious to think or speak of it as grievous.

The law does not require us to regard and treat our Heavenly Father in any respect better than He deserves to be treated, and never better than *we know* He deserves, or than we affirm that we *ought* to treat Him. When we can honestly and conscientiously be satisfied with ourselves as to our treatment of God, He will be satisfied. No one shall ever be able, honestly, to say—"I think Thou requirest me to obey to love Thee more than Thou deservest to be obeyed and loved." There is nothing in either law or gospel which requires anything beyond the legitimate demands of our own reason. Nay more; the law appeals to him in its own vindication and makes his own conscience the rule. God appeals to every moral agent to judge for himself what is right. "Are not My ways equal, says He; are not your ways unequal?" "Of how much sorer punishment, *suppose ye*, shall he be thought worthy, who has trodden under foot the Son of God?" So throughout the Scripture God makes His appeal to man's own mind to judge for himself of the rectitude of the law imposed on him and of the equity of the threatened penalty. Who then should say that the spirit of His government is overbearing, capricious, unreasonable? Who can regard His commandments grievous?

Again, God never requires His interests to be estimated above their real value. Yet some think God to be very selfish, in requiring everybody to love Him. But what less could He require? God does not ask you to love Him more than He deserves to be loved; nor more than it is right you should love Him. This love which God requires of you towards Himself is good-willing, and it has intrinsically for its object the happiness of sentient beings, and should be in proportion to the amount of *being*, so to speak, which each individual may have; or (which amounts to the same result) to the amount of happiness each is capable of enjoying. Now God's capacity for happiness is infinite and therefore is an end of infinite value and rightly claims the utmost good-willing of all created beings. When God asks you to love Him supremely, He only asks you to love Him in proportion to the importance of the object—on His own happiness. If His interests are supreme, why not accord to them your supreme regard?

But He requires of you also the love of complacency; a delight in His character as good. He asks that this should be supreme, and why should He not? Is He not infinitely worthy of your complacency and regard?

Yet further; God never requires us to regard any interest not known, or which we are not capable of knowing; nor does He ask us to regard any interest beyond its perceived or perceivable value. Thus universally, God measures His demands by our powers of obedience, love and service. He never requires us to do things we cannot reach and grasp; never, to treat Him with any more confidence than He deserves, nor to love Him when He is unworthy of our love, or at all beyond His worthiness.

God's requisitions upon us never go beyond our honest convictions of what they should be. He does not require things, the propriety of which is to our own minds questionable. He is never despotic, never tyrannical. His intelligent creatures are always under the conviction that God's will ought to be obeyed and ought to be the universal law. He requires of no creature of His in any world more obedience or love than His own intelligence sees and affirms to be right.

No one can rightly ask of us any more or other feelings than those which naturally result from right intentions and a right state of the will. The feelings, it should be considered, are involuntary and therefore are not directly controlled by the will; yet they are so related to the will that certain feelings naturally follow a right state of the will and certain other feelings, a wrong state. Hence moral responsibility truly attaches to the state of the will; and it is on this principle that

God acts, declaring that "if there be first a willing mind, it is accepted."

In accordance with this, God never requires any other action or course of life except what naturally flows from right intention. Hence He lays His requisitions on the will or heart, requiring only that this be right and thus virtually requiring its natural results and out-flowings.

IV. *What God's law does require.*

An equitable state of mind; one that regards every known interest according to our judgment of its value. God requires us to regard the universal good of each being according to its perceived value. This is an equitable and right state of mind. It is a voluntary and a simple state of mind, a mere unit. Instead of being embarrassed with points of casuistry, it comes to you asking only that you give your heart to God and merge your will in homage to His because His is infinite reason. It simply requires you to regard all interests according to their perceived value. If your neighbors interests are equal to your own, regard them so; if less, regard them less; if greater, regard them more. God never requires any being to sacrifice his own interest for a less valuable interest of another. Hence, when He requires of us universal benevolence, this does not demand that we love others and not ourselves—God and not ourselves; but only each, according to its value. Hence this law never drops from regard our to own interest, but most effectually secures it.

This Christian, virtuous, life, is the natural and certain result of the state of mind which drops selfishness, and puts self and all other interests in their proper places. You have only to maintain that state of mind and abide in it; then your acts and state will meet the entire demands of the law.

Let us now look into the gospel. This requires the same as the law, and something more. It comes, in most inviting and impressive form, to win us back to the love and obedience which the law enjoins. Its special requisition for this end is that we *receive the Holy Ghost* as the condition and means of practical obedience and a practical realization of the great result of holiness in heart and life. Man needs such an influence; therefore God provides it. Whatever else did or did not occur at the fall of man in Eden, it is plain that the Holy Ghost was grieved. Man tore himself away from his God and from communion with Him, so that God no longer dwelt within him. But now God is seeking to restore that state of communion and fellowship. He now returns to man in the person of His Spirit, and asks of the sinner to open his heart and make this Heaven agent welcome.

I need not here speak of the case of those who know not the gospel, only to say that all such are plainly under the law only, and not under the gospel. They have the work of the law written in their heart; and by this light they stand or fall. But of us, who have the gospel, God requires that we should receive the Holy Ghost. Some will say—is not this unreasonable? No; for the Holy Ghost is not far away in some remote quarter of the universe where you cannot reach Him, but is present, and needs only be made welcome and He will take up His abode with you. He comes in connection with His word, to teach, enforce and impress it; and the thing for you to do is to yield yourself to the conviction of the truth, thus revealed. To yield to truth, is to yield to God. When the Bible shows you that you ought to believe and trust God, then to do this is to yield to the Spirit of God and to welcome His presence to your heart. When you know that you ought to give up your sins, then to yield to this conviction is to consent to the claims of His Spirit and to receive it to your soul. Else you resist the Holy Ghost. He does not expect you to rise of yourself and without His aid from the state of death in which you are plunged, but requires you to receive the Holy Ghost, and continually, to yield to every conviction of duty. By presentation of the truth, He draws; you are to yield; He constrains; you acquiesce. He requires you to be led and filled with the Spirit; to lean on Him and to avail yourself of His help. He bids you obey His perfect law; and by this divine agency, offered through the Spirit, He provides all requisite aid and strength for this purpose. This provision is both full and free. If it were otherwise, you might find or feel it hard to be required to be filled with the Holy Ghost. If you must needs ascend into heaven to bring Him down, or descend into the deep to bring Him up, this might be grievous. But only to receive a present and offered Spirit; how can you think this hard? Jesus comes to restore and reinstate you in holiness and love; does He require you to do all this unaided? He neither expects nor requires it. He tenders to you His advocacy; proposes to advocate your cause without cost. Are you rich? Give to your suffering fellow men and please God therein; Are you poor? He requires of you only according to what you have.

He does not require you to live an anxious distracted life, bearing all your own burdens alone, but has permitted you to be "without carefulness," casting all your care upon Him. He gives you the fullest permission to let the peace of God rule in your heart; and is this a hard thing? Is this state of mind a hard and grievous one? Jesus said—"My peace I give unto you; not as the world giveth, give I unto you." The men of the world give sparingly, grudgingly; they give today and take back tomorrow; but not so does Christ give to His friends. Is this grievous?

He says—"Rejoice always." Many seem to think religion only fit for sick-beds and funeral occasions, and they say, "What have we to do with a religion so gloomy? Must we forego all our enjoyments? How grievous that would be!" The "righteous should make their boast in Him and be glad." In His salvation, let them "exceedingly rejoice." God invites them to look up to Him hopefully, never desponding, much less despairing. If He had required you to rejoice in worldly pleasure and be happy in the good things of earth, this were indeed a hard saying and a grievous commandment.

But I have heard some of you say—"God wants nothing to do with me; He has utterly cast me off; How then can I believe and trust in Him? I have abused Him too long." Mark; God asks of you no such feelings, no such thoughts. On the contrary He only asks you to take Him at His word and welcome to your soul a full salvation. He gives you the full consolation of believing. Is this grievous?

He requires you to embrace every dispensation with a kiss; to believe that all things shall work together for your good; and so believing, to rejoice in all your afflictions and tribulations.

Of you, sinner, He requires that you should come today and bring all your load of guilt to Him. Come, however deeply conscious of much past sin; come and hold your soul under the flowing stream of His redeeming blood. And is this hard? Is this too bad? Is it too bad that He should forgive so freely and tender you the waters of life without money or price? He does not require you to hear a great many sermons or make a great many impenitent prayers.

But you say—"Lord, if I were a Christian, I would come at once to Thee; but now, I must certainly make myself better before I come." "No," says your Savior; "come now. Make no delay; offer no excuses for refusal." "Can I come, you say, without His help?" Is He not helping you even now? Suppose I should sit sullenly down and refuse to move, when everything is ready and nothing wanting but the action of my own will? Suppose I should then plead that I lacked the power and that I must wait! What nonsense!

Now He offers you His hand and asks you to take hold of it with your own. There must be a reciprocal taking hold of hands, the Spirit's agency working together with your own. The hand of your faith must take hold of the hand let down from heaven to you. And is this hard or grievous?

REMARKS.

What could God have required less than He does? Nothing. What could He have required which would be more easy? I appeal to every sinner in this house; can you think of anything more easy, more feasible, more available? Of course you cannot think of His saving you in your sins. This would be no salvation. Do you complain that Christ's commands are grievous? In what one particular could He have done better?

You know that Christ has always done as much as He could for your salvation. Can you suggest a better, or more available system? Can you devise anything better than for you to take hold of His strength? He gives you the entire influence of His example, the utmost virtue of His blood and of His dying love; can you think of anything more favorable?

Let me ask these young women, can you think of anything better? Has He made salvation less easy than He might? Did you ever tell Him so? Do you say—"Why did He not over-rule my freedom?" If He had, He could not have saved you any how. Could He have done anything more that would have been of service towards your salvation? Has He refused to make any sacrifices that if made, would have done you good? Did He avoid the cross? Did He shun the shame? Did He stay in heaven and bask in its bliss? Oh *No !* He came down; He *flew* to your relief; although He saw how many groans and how much blood it would cost Him.

Have you thought of any expression of love which He has not made? Of any words of tenderness and forbearance He should have uttered, but did not? Have you acquainted yourself with what He has said? Is it said guardedly? Is the fulfillment uncertain? What is wanting?

How wicked in you if you complain! What have you to complain of? He has done the best He could; and have you any right to complain of that? How wicked to regard and treat His service and His gospel as if it were a hard thing!

A young woman said to me, "I am trying to become a Christian." What does that mean? Real honest trying implies the full consent of the will, and that is all that God requires. This consent is, being converted. People commonly deceive themselves when they talk thus about *trying*.

How great a mistake, to suppose that we cannot obey God. If our circumstances and nature were such that we absolutely *could* not obey Him, it would indeed be very grievous for Him to require it. But how can it be difficult now, since the thing He requires is only right willing? To say that a moral agent tries to will right and yet cannot is a downright absurdity. Nobody ever tried to will right and found it hard. This would be a contradiction in terms.

Inasmuch as the Spirit of God is freely given to us, it must be easy and not hard for us to get it. The command therefore to "be filled with the Spirit" is by no means grievous.

Only those complain of its being difficult to obey the law who would fain do it without accepting the help offered in the gospel. With the heart all wrong, they try to render an external obedience. This is always a hard up-hill business.

Without being at all aware of it many are trying to get along without Christ. Their effort is to make themselves good enough by dint of resolutions and efforts of their own, made quite in their own strength. Such persons, of course, will find it hard to be religious.

In a little different mode, some try to get grace by works of love. They want to come to Christ, but in order to get Christ, they try to work up a certain state of feeling and perform some legal works. All this is quite aside from the simplicity of gospel faith.

In like manner many try to get the Spirit without yielding to His present teachings. Overlooking and disobeying these, they wait for more light and pray for more of the Holy Spirit, while they refuse to obey what they have.

In fact, such persons fail to use a present offered Savior; do not realize how near, and how free, and how rich, are His gifts, nor how truly they are available—that they may as truly have and use the strength of Christ as they can use the strength of their own muscles. You may hear them crying and shouting aloud for the Holy Ghost, as if He were as far off as the fixed stars, not aware that He is really *within them,* trying to bring them to take hold of His present help. Such people make religion a hard and grievous matter. They do not understand its great simplicity and its ineffable richness and adaptation to human want.

Those who refuse to take Christ at His word will find it hard to get religion. You will hear them saying—

> "Reason I hear, her counsels weigh,
> And all I hear I approve;
> But still I find it hard t'obey,
> And harder still to love."

Is that your experience? If so, then you do not believe one word of Christ's promises. You have failed to reach the simplicity of gospel faith. While Christ is trying by every means to woo and to wed your heart to Himself, and lets down an almighty arm to rescue and save you, what reception does He meet with! Each Sabbath evening in this place, we meet persons who think it one of the hardest things in the world to become Christians; who say—"I am trying to find Christ, but I must conclude He is not to be found. I cannot come to Him." Are not all these conceptions of Christ unkind to Him? Are they not false, injurious to Christ?

The great mass of professors of religion take ground directly opposed to our text. Whereas the inspired word declares—"His commandments are not grievous," they represent God's service as very hard and full of grief. Reason; they are in legal bondage, and have never broken out into the glorious liberty of the children of God. Let me ask these sinners, have you not received the impression from what you have heard Christians say, that it is a very difficult thing to get religion and that its service is so hard and God's law so high, it requires an angel's heart to keep it? Whereas the truth is, God requires nothing in anywise unreasonable. It is easier to be well-disposed than ill-disposed. How then can you say, it is easier to rebel that to obey? O sinner, all such notions are utterly false. His commandments are not grievous.

Look at that young man who says—"If I become a Christian I shall be compelled to preach the gospel, and O, what dull work and poor pay!" Does he forget that they who "turn many to righteousness shall shine as the stars forever and ever?" Is this too hard?

But he says—"I must be a missionary and go to Africa; be sick there and die an early death." Well; "he that will lose his life for My sake, the same shall save it."

"But I am not eloquent." Oh, not eloquent! Can you not stammer out the gospel story? If it were really in your heart filling all your soul with its rich experience, could you not give some utterance to its glorious yet simple message? Beware of ambition! If you could be the first preacher in all the land—the most eloquent and the most applauded, that would do! Oh, that unholy ambition! You make your religion insufferably hard if you try to serve both God and your own ambition!

Chapter III.

PRAYER FOR A PURE HEART.

Reported by Rev. Henry Cowles. March 14, 1849.

"Create in me a clean heart, O God, and renew a right spirit within me."

Psalm 51: 10.

The term rendered "right" in this passage is in the margin, *constant*, and this seems to be its precise meaning. A constant, stedfast spirit, as opposed to the fickle and unstable state in which he had so sadly fallen before temptation, was the thing he now desired and sought in earnest prayer.

In discussing the subject brought before us in this passage, I shall,

I. Show what this petition really means.

II. What is implied in offering it acceptably.

I. The terms *heart* and *spirit* are used in the Bible in various senses. The term *heart* often denotes the *will*, or the voluntary attitude or state of the will. Sometimes it is opposed to flesh, and then is synonymous with *mind* as distinct from body. In our text, both heart and spirit seem to be used in their widest and most general sense, including the whole mind—not its voluntary powers and states only, but also those which are involuntary. We must suppose that these terms as here used, include other powers than the will, for it is manifest that his will was substantially in a right state already. He did not regard his will as opposed to God, for his will goes out in this earnest, and apparently most sincere prayer that his whole being might be made pure, and be put in such a state that he should never sin again. It lies on the very face of this psalm that David's will was right before God. Hence he prays for something which he calls a clean heart and a right spirit, which is more than merely a right state of the will—which may be wisely sought in prayer after one's will is subdued, humbled, yielded to God and submissive. Of course a clean heart and a right spirit, as here used, imply a thorough cleansing or sanctification of the whole mind; including the regulation, or cleansing of the imagination, the thoughts, desires, feelings—all those modifications of the sensibility, and all those habitudes of thought and feeling which so often annoy the Christian and become most distressing and dangerous snares to his soul. These are often spoken of in the Bible as fleshly—"fleshly lusts that war against the soul." David obviously prays that God would do for him all that his omniscient eye saw needful to make and keep himself pure from all sin, forever. He prays to be *made right* throughout all the powers and habitudes of his being.

II. *What is implied in offering it acceptably?*

1. That it be offered *intelligently*. The supplicant must understand what he needs, and have a practical and just apprehension of it. There can be no real prayer without this.

2. This implies, of course, a *deep conviction of past sin*. One who is not convicted by the Holy Ghost has no conception of what this language means. Indeed, without the illumination and convicting agency of the Spirit, the sinner has no right conceptions of any thing of a spiritual nature. Hence, he needs to be convicted, so as to understand thoroughly the nature of sin; then he will see his need, and *feel* it deeply. This deep feeling, based on a just apprehension of his sin and guilt, is essential to acceptable prayer for a clean heart.

3. A sincere offering of this prayer implies sincere repentance—a real turning of the will from all sin; for without this there can not be sincere prayer for a clean heart.

4. It implies, also, confession of sin to God. By this I mean more than simply uttering our acknowledgment of sins before God; I mean confessing them *as sins committed against God*, deeply realizing the power and self-application of David's

words—"Against thee, thee only have I sinned, and done this evil in thy sight." Now it is easy, and cheap too, for some men to confess their sins, but truly to understand the nature of sin in its relations to God—to see how odious and how abominably guilty one's own sin is in view of these relations; this is much more than mere oral confession. And yet the suppliant must enter deeply into those views of sin, and realize that for his great sins against God he deserves the divine wrath forever, or he can not throw his whole soul into this prayer for a clean heart and a right spirit.

5. There must also be a deep apprehension of one's danger of falling under temptation. It is plain that David in praying for a clean heart and a right spirit, made use of popular language, but really referred to those things in his constitution and habits which had been to him *occasions* of great sin. Who does not know that after the will is set right, and has done all it can do towards consecrating the whole being to God, the occasions of sin still exist, and may still act with great energy. For example, the imagination, long trained in the course of sin, long corrupted, polluted, filled with foul images, and terribly under the control of impure associations —this remains to be regulated, renovated, and as we might well say, *cleansed*, before it can be otherwise than a snare, and a most unfit associate of a right will.

It should however be understood that sin, strictly speaking, belongs to acts of the *will* only; and that of course, when sin or moral defilement is predicated of other faculties or states of the mind, the language is used in a popular and not a metaphysical sense. While this is true and important to be understood, it still remains true also that our mental associations, our habitudes of both mind and body have been during our life of sin such that they continue after conversion to be active and fruitful occasions of sin. This is illustrated in the case of David. His imagination had not become so regulated, nor had his passions been so crucified and sanctified as to cease to act as occasions and temptations to sin. His lusts and appetites had long been so indulged and so developed by indulgence, that though his will was converted to God, yet it might still be overpowered by their temptations. Every Christian knows more or less of the presence and power of these temptations. He is also conscious that these appetites, feelings, passions, imaginations and habitudes create within the mind a certain uneasiness and sense of loathing as if they were really unclean.

The Bible speaks of "the motions of sins," while we are in the flesh, as "working in our members to bring forth fruit unto death," and it would seem to speak of them in popular language as being sinful. As to the case of David, whoever has had experience in the government of a vitiated sensibility, and of indulged passion, can not read this psalm without seeing what were the workings of his mind. Deeply convicted of his great sin, his mind turns within upon those propensities of such fearful power—those appetites and habitudes, and those workings of a vile imagination which had so woefully ensnared his soul and dishonored his God, and he cries aloud—O, my God, give me a pure heart— "Create in me a clean heart, O God, and renew a right spirit within me. Wash me thoroughly from mine iniquity, and cleanse me from my sin."

Hence this prayer implies, as I said, a clear apprehension of those things which become occasions of sin, and involve especially a request for their entire subjugation and cleansing.

Those of you who have read Madame Guyon, noticed that in speaking of the great work wrought in her, she alludes to the fact that her imagination had been greatly polluted, but was at length, through sanctifying grace, so brought under the power of a holy will, as to be no longer a source of conflict as before, so in the case of all Christians, the correction of all these habitudes of mind and wayward imaginings and physical propensities constitutes an important part of the work of moral cleansing.

6. This prayer offered acceptably implies a loathing of these occasions of sin and a deep dread of them. Take, for example, the man who has a polluted imagination. If he be a Christian, will he not find this an occasion of great self-loathing? Deeply ashamed of himself, he often feels as if it would be a relief to him if he could spue out his very self—all those vile pollutions of thought and imagination— and be a new and pure creature. For although the action of the imagination is not itself sin, not being directly a voluntary state of mind, yet it often becomes a most disgusting and loathsome *occasion* of sin, and consequently in the renewed mind an occasion of great conflict. Hence the strong desire to be made pure in these respects.

7. It involves also an apprehension of our dependence on God to subdue those habitudes of sin. Every one who has tried to manage them himself has learned his own weakness; but ordinarily men learn their weakness and dependence no faster than they gain this experience by efforts to master these propensities to sin. How often does the Christian find himself thrown in to deep agonizing, struggling and struggling a long time perhaps in vain to gain the fixed ascendency over all within which creates temptations and occasions to sin! When this painful and dear-bought experience has thoroughly taught a man his dependence on God, he can then sincerely ask God to do this great work of moral cleansing for him. Without the teachings of experience, you can scarcely expect any man to be so sincere and heartily earnest in praying as to prevail. It seems indispensable that every Christian should know, past all doubt or demurring, that he needs God's aid, and can do nothing to the purpose without it.

8. This prayer also implies a confidence in the ability of God to do this work. It is a most remarkable fact that nearly the whole church has embraced the opinion that *death* must do this work. I speak now only of the masses of professed Christians, for some individuals hold different views, and pray

as David did for entire moral cleansing to take place here in time. There is no evidence in this Psalm that David prayed or expected death to do this work; on the other hand he most obviously prayed for a work to be done here and now, and himself expected to live after it was done, and tells God what he shall do after his heart is made clean in answer to his prayers. "Then," says, he, "will I teach transgressors thy ways, and sinners shall be converted unto thee."

But most Christians in these latter ages of the world have expected and do expect death to do this work, and of course they expect nothing better than to carry along all these loathsome things till they die. A hard lot this, if indeed it were an allotment of Jehovah; but a strange lot for a Christian to impose upon himself by failing to embrace the proffer of almighty aid, in the speedy accomplishment of a universal renewal unto holiness.

Certain others have thought that subduing the propensities is equivalent to their annihilation. This, however is a great mistake; for David who prayed that his whole being might be cleansed, evidently did not expect to lose his imagination altogether, nor indeed did he think of having any other faculty of mind or body annihilated, as if God had created some faculties which are intrinsically evil, and must therefore be expunged from the system before it can be morally pure! Not so, I say, did David think and pray; but on the contrary he prayed virtually that God would regenerate his whole being—overhaul it—make it over, mold it into purity and order, till it should subserve, and not derange the right action of a sanctified will.

9. This prayer implies confidence not only that God is *able* to answer it, but also not less that He is *willing*, and moreover that to do it is in accordance with the plans and purposes of his moral government. If he had only believed that God is able, but that He has no purpose, plan or will to do such a thing, under any circumstances of our earthly life, would it not have

been blasphemous for him to have offered this prayer? Look at it! Suppose David had believed as some now are understood to hold, that God, though able, had no intention or will to give the Christian a clean heart during this life, would not this prayer of his have been impious? It would be as much as to say—Lord I know thou hast no desire or intention to give thy children a pure heart in this world; but, Lord, we want this blessing, and we want it *now*, and we can not be denied—let thy purposes stand ever so much opposed to granting the blessing. Now could the Psalmist have offered such a prayer without tempting God? Certainly not. Hence we may infer that he doubtless believed it to be in accordance with God's government and plans to bestow this blessing when earnestly sought by prayer.

I have often known men who had great misgivings whether God did not intend, in all cases, to leave Christians through life impure—their hearts not cleansed in the sense of our text. Consequently if they ever ask for these blessings, they are afraid to believe, and hence they can not possibly cast themselves upon the Lord in such confidence as is essential to prevailing prayer. They know that God is able, but they do not believe Him willing; hence they are greatly troubled, and there can be no strong confidence, no child-like trust in their prayers.

Not so David. Plainly he held God to be willing as well as able. You must certainly admit that David assumed God's willingness to do the very thing he asked, whatever you may suppose that thing to be. The real thing requested in his prayer, he must have supposed God most willing to perform.

10. The sincere offering of the prayer that God would create in us a clean heart implies that on our part *we are willing to have the thing done*. Persons often have strong desires that something were done, who yet are not willing it should be done. A tooth aches bitterly; they know it ought to come out; O, how they wish it were out now—but are they *willing* to have it done? That's the trying point. Their desires in the

matter are very strong, but don't amount to a willingness. So, often, in regard to wishing and praying for a clean heart. It often happens that persons think they want a pure heart; but when they come to see all that is implied in it, they shrink back, and say, *no;* we can not meet all those consequences. A striking case of this sort once fell under my observation. A young lady claimed she was willing to become a Christian, and I suppose honestly thought so, I often pressed her with the fact that she was not really willing to become a Christian, but she as often resisted my position and my arguments. Ultimately she heard a sermon which greatly affected her, and brought her to determine that she would not live in her sins any longer. She turned her thoughts in deep earnest towards God—she began to ask Him to take away all her sins—when suddenly she saw so clearly how much would be involved in this, that she shrunk back—withdrew her petition—rose from her knees and went her way. She had found that she did not want to be *such a Christian.*

So, often, with professed Christians. When they see all that is implied in a clean heart, they turn away. They may have offered this prayer often without at all apprehending how much it implies. When they come to see the whole matter they are conscious of shrinking from meeting such results.

Hence an acceptable offering of this prayer implies that we are willing to have this whole work done—are willing to have every constitutional appetite, passion, tendency and function of either flesh or spirit so modified as to come perfectly under the control of right reason, and of God's revealed will. We must be willing to have our bodies become fit temples for God's indwelling Spirit; every function or faculty of our entire nature being in harmony with a holy heart, being such as would not soil an angel's purity, if his spirit were to inhabit our body, and act through our physical organs.

11. This prayer offered acceptably, implies that we are willing God should do his own work *in his own way.*

It often happens that really men dictate to God the manner in which things shall be done. They ask only with certain reservations and qualifications—as if they would say—May God be pleased to do this thing provided it shall not touch my idol; my God sanctify all my appetites, so as to bring them under the law of enlightened reason, except this favorite one—spare me this, for I am very partial to it, and it has been such a comfort to me so long! Or perhaps they are afraid to pray right out—without qualification or exception, that God would actually give them a heart universally clean, and a spirit altogether right, lest, if their prayer should be answered it might smite some of the precious things they love. As a woman once said to me—"I dare not ask for sanctification, lest if I should, *God should take away my husband!*" "But why such fears?" "Because I am conscious that my heart is greatly bound up in him, and I am terribly afraid that God could not sanctify me without tearing him away from my heart."

Of course the woman could not pray—"Create in me a clean heart, O God, and renew a right spirit within me." This prayer implies that we are willing to have any sacrifice made which God sees to be necessary; that we yield up ourselves to all the outward training, and also to all the inward training which in the eye of God may appear to be requisite. We submit ourselves to his discretion as to the things to be done—as to the time, the manner, and all the circumstances of doing it. We do most fully and freely consent that God should use his own infinite wisdom. Let Him smite whatever he sees it best to smite. Let my soul commit itself into his hands to suffer any pain, and endure any sacrifice which his wisdom may choose and his love can inflict. Let me never fear any unreasonable severity *from such a Father!*

But how often Christians have their own way marked out for God to walk in. They would have Him be careful to deal with themselves very gently, and especially beware not to use his providential rod too roughly. It would suit them well if the

Lord would come down upon them as with an electric shock and shake their very souls into purity and holiness. Some sudden and purely spiritual agency is often the thing they are dreaming of, and they prefer that the clean heart shall come in this way rather than by any form of sore trial. They seem not to realize that there are some attachments of such a character that God can not rectify them without seizing upon the loved object, cutting it down, tearing up its very roots, and rending asunder all those tender ligaments which bind our hearts in selfish, idolatrous love to our idol. Every Christian ought to consider that asking God sincerely to create in us a clean heart involves the submission of our entire case to his management, with full permission from us to use the *knife*, or any thing else He may find necessary for a thorough cure.

12. This prayer, to be acceptable, must involve not only a willingness to have the thing done, but to take with it the consequences which will naturally follow. If the gift of a clean heart involves new relations and new duties, we must meet them cheerfully, and what is more, in anticipation of them we must not shrink; for if we do, we can not have the gift. Thus, for example, it is obviously the duty of those whom God thus blesses to glorify his name. Let them, like the ancient leper, go into the temple to bear their public testimony to saving grace. Or, like David let them be able to say—"I have not *hid* thy righteousness within my heart, I have not concealed thy loving-kindness and thy truth from the great congregation." Even beforehand let them say as he did—"Deliver me, and my tongue shall sing aloud of thy righteousness;" "open thou my lips, and my mouth shall show forth thy praise."

Now many would be very willing to be religious, if they might accomplish it all without any consequent reproach. They might even be happy to be sanctified if they might have the blessing with no attendant dishonor—no sacrifice of reputation; if nobody would talk about them—if none would observe their conduct and their spirit more closely than before.

But all such compromises for reputation's sake are vain and ruinous. You must be willing to lay your very self upon God's altar—yourself I say, your all; reputation, name, ease, your estate if need be, your personal liberty if God's providence calls for it, and even your life. Go up with firm, unfaltering step and lay your all upon that altar; then let God do with that offering what He will;—blast it—burn it—blow it to every quarter of the heavens; yet lay it down and say, whether in the fear or the fact of all losses—"These thing are thine, O my God—do with them all as thou pleasest. Spare me nothing which thou pleasest to take. I trust thy wisdom and thine infallible love." Now every Christian should know that the gift of a clean heart and a right spirit comes not from God till he is willing to take with it its legitimate consequences—nay more, till he is willing to trust those results to the wisdom of his great Father. You must be willing to be made a spectacle to angels and to men, for God will never light a candle to put it under a bushel. You may lift up your cry the hundredth time for the blessing; still the question will return—Will you glorify God? Will you let your light shine? Will you do all you can to make the gift, if bestowed on you, available to the glory of the Blessed Giver? God asks—Are you willing I should put you in the furnace and heat up the fire to seven-fold fury, and let the world look on to see what grace can do? You greatly mistake if you suppose God does such works of sanctifying mercy for your sake alone. "Not for *your* sake, be it known unto you, O house of Israel, saith the Holy One, but for my holy name's sake." (Ezk. 36)

Let it then be well understood that you must be willing to meet and bear the trials which God sends. You must expect trials, such trials as will probably call the attention of others to your case. God perhaps would fain profit others by the blessings He gives you. If so, should you rebel? Perhaps He would glorify Himself. If so, shall you shrink? Never. It becomes you rather to glory in tribulation, outward or inward—for it is sweet even by suffering, to be made the passive instruments of glorifying our Father in heaven. Let the burning trial come, if the grace of God thereby shines the more brightly. It is the manner of our God to make the holiness of his people and the riches of his own grace shine most gloriously in the furnace of affliction.

REMARKS.

1. I remark first what I have already said in substance but repeat here, that David intended to be sanctified in the present life. His will at the time of his offering the prayer in the text was already right, but he had others things about him which were not right, and his soul was fixed to have them corrected. His vile imagination must be regulated—his lusts subdued and slain. He wanted the whole man set in such tone that he should not be forever falling before temptation. All these were blessings which he needed in the present life if ever—needed *then*—which moreover he prayed he might obtain *then*, and which he manifestly expected then.

2. Many are in the habit of using this language of prayer frequently without really apprehending what it means. Consequently their prayers obtain no particular answer. No man need expect a specific answer to prayer unless he prays for something specific and knows what it is. It is impossible that there should be intelligent desire for objects unless those objects are apprehended by the mind with considerable distinctness.

3. Many do not fulfill the conditions so as offer the prayer acceptably. They lack the requisite confidence in God. Not asking in faith, they can not receive, for their unbelief places it beyond the power of God to bless them without sacrificing his own honor.

4. We do not understand the recorded prayers of Scripture, nor the promises, until we are brought into a state of mind similar to that of the writer. Recurring to the case of David, I do not mean that none can understand his prayer in our text

until they have committed David's sins; but I do mean that we must see ourselves to have committed some sins, and that we must be greatly humbled and deeply penitent as he was—be filled with utter self-loathing as was the case with him. Such a state of mind brings out the full and precious meaning of the promise; it unfolds it like a charm, in lustre and glory such as none but the humbled soul can possibly appreciate.

It is moreover quite essential that we should understand our liabilities to fall before temptation. Probably David, before his sin, was not aware of his great danger—did not know how powerful those occasions to sin actually were. He might have been entirely unaware that any circumstances could ever have involved in such dreadful sin—first seduction and adultery; then betrayal and murder in their meanest form; who can believe that David, anterior to his sin, understood all his own fearful liabilities to such sins as these? What, therefore, must have been his amazement when these terrible tendencies and occasions of sin came to be developed! How did he then cry out in the deep anguish of his soul—"O my God, save me from myself! O my God, create in me a clean heart, and renew a right spirit within me." So must every Christian see himself in these dark, fearful aspects of his character, before his prayer will be, like David's, a prayer of deep agony of soul.

5. It is not uncommon for Christians to have a right will and of course be in this respect acceptable to God while yet their previous habits have been so bad as to subject them to continual struggles and warfare; the imagination taking its filthy course and rioting in its pollutions unless constantly held in check by the pressure of some great considerations. Now the thing needed by such persons is to see their dangers and liabilities, and then to throw themselves upon the saving strength of the Most High.

6. The unsanctified, involuntary states of mind are great enemies to the soul. These appetites are the "fleshly lusts" that war against the soul's peace and purity. If these were removed

there would still remain the devil to war against; with them we have both Satan from without, and our unsubdued propensities and ungoverned imagination within.

Formerly it was supposed that these conflicts with appetite were a real warfare with inborn and inbred sin. I hold no such doctrine. These appetites are not themselves sin, but they are the occasions of sin—the means of temptation to sin, and hence are objects of dread and loathing to the Christian.

7. In proportion as these lusts are subdued, there will arise in the mind a sense of purity. I have said that the soul loathes these appetites and passions which become occasions of sin, and loathes itself on account of them and their vile associations. For the same reasons, when purified from these loathed abominations, there will ensue a sweet consciousness of being pure, such as can by no means exist prior to their subjugation and cleansing.

8. This rectification of the appetites, sensibilities and imagination, has been commonly called sanctification, because men have really supposed that these things were themselves sinful. If they really were so, then their rectification would be genuine sanctification. In popular language there seems to be no strong objection to their being so called now. Indeed the Bible, ever using popular language, speaks of sanctification as affecting "spirit, soul and body." "The very God of peace sanctify you wholly. And I pray God your whole spirit and soul and body be preserved *blameless*" —as if blame might attach to either. The writer doubtless intends simply the sanctification of the whole man—in which state the body would no longer become the occasion of sin to the mind.

9. This blessing is exceedingly valuable and desirable. It is hardly possible to estimate adequately its great value. Let one experience what David did—have reason to loathe himself as he had; have occasion to know the dreadful power of those inward foes—those terrible snares to his soul;—let him see how his tyrant lusts have overpowered him and laid him

prostrate and bleeding in the dust;—then may he see how greatly desirable it is to have even the hottest fires of providential discipline seize upon him and burn up all his tin and all his dross, till nothing remains but gold well purified. O how he will rejoice even through such a process to come forth redeemed, and cleansed, so that he may stand henceforth perfect and complete in all the will of God!

10. This blessing is indispensable to inward tranquility and peace of mind. In no farther than this entire work is advanced, can one enjoy repose in God. The will may be right; but the mind will almost continually experience those terrible agitations which result from conflict with unsubdued, ungoverned sensuality. There can be no abiding peace till the whole man is brought into harmony with God's service—with a holy will and a holy life.

11. Especially is this blessing greatly desirable as a condition of passing tranquilly through sore outward trials. When men have received this blessing, it seems to be the order of God's providence to test them, and cause them to exhibit great calmness, to the praise of victorious grace. Then observers will wonder how they can pass so calmly and so sweetly through trials so fiery. As the three children in Daniel walked within the burning furnace, amid its hottest flames, and when they came forth no smell of fire had been on them, for the Son of God had been with them there—so when Christians have their lusts subdued and slain before hand—so that Jesus can walk with them through the furnace, no fires can burn upon them from without, nor from within. All is calm and all is safe. Said a man once of a Christian sister who was under most distressing trials—"I wonder how she can live." But she was calm and quiet as a lamb. God can purify us so that we can pass through the most terrific trials unruffled as the air of a summer evening.

12. This state is greatly important to our highest usefulness. Men have been useful without this; but if they would be useful in the highest degree they must go to God imploring him to

do all He sees they need. This is the very spirit in which we should apply to God for this blessing. "O my God, do all thy will in me; then put me in any position in the universe which will most fully illustrate and extol thy grace. No matter what it be, only let it greatly glorify thy name."

13. Until this work is done, Christians will, more or less frequently, be a great stumbling-block to the world, and indeed to all others. So was David. His heart was not thoroughly made pure; hence a constant liability to such dreadful sins as those into which he fell. Pres. Edwards made, and put on record this most excellent resolution;—"When I fall into any sins, I will not rest until I have searched out and found the occasion and have removed it." This great man had learned enough from his own experience to show him that he must look for the *occasions of sin*. When a patient is sick you would not attack the symptoms, but would look for the occasions or causes and would seek to remove them; so in the occurrence of sin, you must look for the occasions and give yourself no rest till they are thoroughly removed. Hence the fitness of this prayer made by the Psalmist—and hence the reason why you should go to God and cry, "O my God create in me a clean heart;—take away all these distressing occasions of sin, or I shall continue to dishonor thee and bring reproach on thy name."

Chapter IV.

OPEN THOU MINE EYES!

July 17, 1844.

"Open Thou mine eyes that I may behold wondrous things out of Thy law."

Ps. 119: 18.

In this discourse I shall show—
I. IN WHAT SENSE THE TERM LAW IS USED IN THE TEXT.
II. THE MEANING OF THE REQUEST—"OPEN THOU MINE EYES."
III. WHAT IS IMPLIED IN MAKING THE REQUEST.
IV. THE CONSEQUENCES OF RECEIVING AN ANSWER TO THE REQUEST.
V. THE CONDITION OF AN ANSWER TO THE REQUEST.

I. In what sense the term Law is used in the text.

The term *'law'* is used in various senses in the Bible. Sometimes it means that which was written on the two tables of stone; sometimes the ceremonial law given to Israel by God through Moses; sometimes the five books of Moses in distinction from the books of the prophets and the Psalms, &c.; and sometimes it means the *whole revealed will of God*. This last is its widest sense, and this I suppose to be the meaning in the text; to wit: the whole Old Testament Scriptures—that is, the whole revealed will of God. The prayer of the Psalmist is as if he had said—Open Thou mine eyes to behold wondrous things in the *Bible*.

II. The meaning of the request—"Open thou mine eyes."

1. It does *not* mean create new eyes for me. Nor,
2. Does the Psalmist pray for any physical operation as removing a cataract, or taking away a film from the surface of

the eye; for it is not the natural eye with which we see spiritual things. But,

3. The Psalmist does intend to pray for spiritual light. A man may have good eyes, bodily and mental, and yet he will perceive nothing if light be wanting. I suppose the Psalmist to pray for spiritual light, the medium of spiritual vision, by which, supplied by the in-dwelling Spirit, he may apprehend the wondrous things really revealed in the Bible. Many will inquire—What is this spiritual light? I answer, that I cannot tell what it is, any more than I can tell what natural light is. Ask me what natural light is, and I cannot tell. I can tell what philosophers speculate about it, and that is all. I know this, that in its absence I cannot see, and that in its presence I can see. So there is spiritual light. What it is I know not, but that there is such a thing I do know, (and what Christian does not know it?) Every man enlightened by the Spirit of God knows the fact full well. He may be ignorant of its nature of the manner of its operations, as we doubtless are of both natural and spiritual light, but of the fact of the existence of both we may be perfectly sure; and of the existence of spiritual light, he upon whose eyes it has shone, is as certain as any man can be of the existence of the sun in the heavens. He knows that in its presence he can discern spiritual objects, and that in its absence they are hid from his eyes. Now I say, that the Psalmist in the text, expresses his desire to have spiritual light—his desire for the Spirit to shed his light upon the Bible, without which, he could not see and apprehend the truth of the Bible, and by which, they might be made to stand forth as actual realities to his soul. I pass to show

III. What is implied in the request.

1. It is implied that we possess the faculties requisite for the perception of spiritual objects. The Psalmist prays for no change or new creation, and there needs no change in the nature or organization of our faculties.

2. That our spiritual eyes are useless without light—that they are of no avail till God opens them, or till He supplies the light by which alone we can see—that we shall not and cannot behold the wondrous things in God's law, only as the medium of vision is supplied.

3. That the Psalmist knew very well that there were wonderful things concealed from his spiritual eye in the absence of spiritual light. He knew some of the things contained in the Scriptures doubtless. His eyes had been opened perhaps, and more than once. Indeed, no spiritual man can read the 119 Psalm with any good degree of attention, and not feel that he who wrote it had drank, and that deeply, into the spirit of God's holy law. Every verse almost, nay every verse but two, expresses in some way his love for God's law, the importance of God's law, or the glory of God's law. And the knowledge he already had gained had ravished his heart and made him cry out more earnestly to have his eyes *fully* opened, that he might be able to see clearly the glories of the Scriptures. The Psalmist had without doubt been enabled to get in some degree, behind the veil of types and shadows of the Old Testament, he had taken a peep beneath the drapery, and had seen Christ revealed and the wonderful things of salvation; he had looked through and beyond the outward types and shadows and the sight had so enraptured his soul, that he prayed with agonizing earnestness and importunity—"Open mine eyes. O Lord open Thou mine eyes that I may behold wondrous things out of Thy law." The wonders are in the Bible if we could only see them. We might be walking in the midst of the splendors of nature, and see nothing if there were not light. What are the glories of vision to a blind man? He may encircle the globe, go over its mountains and through its valleys, cross its oceans and its continents, pass among all it beauties and its luxuriance, and yet see nothing. Without eyes they are nothing; or with eyes if there be no light, all is midnight darkness. It is so as to spiritual things. Read the

Bible, pass through its paragraphs, go over its pages, and you may after all see nothing of its beauties—like a man traversing a country in a stage-coach at midnight, he can get nothing of its scenery, how picturesque soever it may be. When men with eyes not opened in the sense of the text read the Bible, they do not see its beauties, do not behold the wondrous things which are nevertheless contained therein, and they should with all earnestness make the prayer of the Psalmist. He prayed because he felt there were things in the law of God which he had never seen.

4. It is implied that we need to know the wonderful things which are spoken of. It is not to be supposed that the Psalmist wished to gratify a vain curiosity. Did he utter this inspired prayer, I ask you, merely from idle curiosity? No. He needed to know, and he felt it; he perishingly needed knowledge, and he cried in view thereof, and not for his own benefit alone, but that he might teach others also, that he might declare the praises of God in the great congregation.

5. It is implied that none but God can open our eyes. The Psalmist knew that a mere knowledge of language, of grammar and philology could avail him nothing. He understood the language of the Scriptures well enough. He did not pray to be taught the language of the Bible, to have the ability to decipher all the philology thereof—he would not pour contempt upon these, but value them in their place. But after all, with all his knowledge of the language, he felt that not any man, not even the wisest, not an angel, could give him the light. No, none but God, none but God by the Spirit which indicted the sacred pages could open his eyes, and hence his prayer to God—'Open Thou mine eyes.' It should never be forgotten that the Bible is a mere dead letter except to those to whom the Spirit makes it a personal revelation. Do you understand me? What did the Psalmist pray for? To *read* the Bible? He could read it. To understand the *words?* He could define them. To become acquainted with the literature of the Bible? No, he

knew all these things well enough. What then? That God would make the Bible a special and personal revelation to him. Not through Moses and the prophets, not by having the Scriptures in his hands, but to *him*, for himself—not by giving light to others, but directly to him—by opening *his* eyes. Lord 'open Thou *mine* eyes.' People are mistaken who think that the Bible is a revelation to them in any such sense as to save their souls, except their eyes are opened by the Holy Ghost. The Psalmist himself could not see without this, and he prayed God to supply to him that light, by the aid of which he might apprehend the truths of God's word. He sees the words—he reads the sentences—but what is the *meaning*? What are the things said? Open my eyes that I may see them. His prayer was to God for he felt that none but God could supply his need. But I hasten to notice,

IV. *The consequences of having our eyes opened in the sense of the text.*

1. *Ourselves* will be revealed. We shall see our own portrait drawn in a manner that will convince us instantly that the pencil of the Omniscient has done the work. It will be as if you had been sitting in the blaze of the Omniscient eye. The clearness and exactness will be startling. You will seem never to have seen yourself before, you will be astonished at the fearful fidelity with which every feature will be sketched. Sinner, let your eyes be opened, and you will have another view of yourself altogether. Though it never entered into your heart to sit for your portrait, yet there is drawn every lineament, there you are, your face blazing right out, staring upon you, every feature and lineament blazing from the page of inspiration. Look where you will, there you are—a vile sinner, and you will wish to flee and get away from the horrible picture of your own face.

2. *God* will be revealed. God and yourself—and this in proportion to the degree of light. If the light be obscure, you will see indistinctly—'men as trees walking'—like moon-light

or star-light. In the star-light you can see the fences, the trees, and the houses; in moonlight you can distinguish more; but yet things are not clear. As the sun approaches, as it puts out the stars and makes the moon dim, as it rises more and more till it appears in perfect day, your view growns fuller and clearer till the whole landscape is bathed in a flood of light. God is revealed—Father, Son, and Holy Ghost—but especially the Son, Christ, is revealed. You will find Christ in places without number, in passages where before you never dreamed Christ was to be found. The more I read my Bible and pray the prayer of our text the more am I convinced of the spirituality of those who find Christ revealed every where in the Bible. Once I thought differently. I remember a few years ago reading Edwards' Notes on the Bible, and that I thought him visionary because he found Christ hinted at so often. He saw Christ every where. I saw no such thing. So some writers will find clear proofs of the divinity of Christ, where others can see no reference thereto at all. Now the difficulty with me was, I lacked spiritual light, so that I was unable to see what was really revealed in the Bible. The Jews, the great body of them, could not see Christ in the Jewish law, they did not see the drift and bent of the Scriptures. Why not? They were carnal, sensual, they had not the Spirit. Where persons' eyes are thus opened, they will have revelations of Christ such as to surprise them exceedingly; such a fullness and glory as will astonish them greatly. O what love! And in proportion to the clearness of the light of the Spirit, you will see that the design of the Bible every where, is to reveal Christ directly or indirectly. Christ is the subject, and the end—in history, in prophecy, in poetry, the Old Testament and the New—every where, Christ is the Alpha and the Omega, the sum and the substance, the beginning and the end. Let your eyes be opened, and Christ is every where—our righteousness, our wisdom, our sanctification, and our redemption.

3. We shall differ very much in our views from all those whose eyes have not been opened. Impenitent young men, you sympathize with each other, you are alike self-wise and vain, you meet and scoff at religion and religious men, you agree in your notion that all piety is superstition and beneath your notice. But let the Spirit open the eyes of one of your number, and how changed his tone. How he will differ from those with whom he so perfectly agreed but just now in his views of himself and of them, of his works and their works, of his relations to God and of theirs. He can no longer sympathize with them, and join their wicked scoffings—he sees with a strong light, and is astonished at their darkness and his former darkness—he shuns them as the gate of hell. Why? His eyes are opened to behold eternity, and the judgment, and his sins. He sees himself, and them, standing upon the slippery steep, and fiery billows rolling beneath, and he cries out, and flees in terror. All this may be true while he is impenitent. But suppose he is converted; then he differs from them still more. He goes farther and farther and farther from them, and as he progresses in grace, and the light of the Spirit's illumination beams stronger and brighter upon his soul, he presses on to the perfect day, while they remain where they were or plunge into deeper darkness.

This difference in views is true moreover of the different stages of Christian experience. As a man's eyes are opened more and more, he differs more and more from those who are below him; he sees things which they cannot see, and has a clear view of what they see but dimly. His view differs from theirs, as a view in the bright noon-day differs from one at evening twilight. Their experience will differ from his, as the description of a village, or a mountain, or a landscape, seen in the evening, would differ from a description of them as seen under broad day-light. Just as far as we get our eyes open we view the Scriptures differently, as naturally as cause produces its effect. As our light increases, our views must enlarge and expand of course. We must see more and better surely, when we stand with the great sun pouring upon our heads his flood of light, than when in the dim star-light we cast our eyes abroad.

And here let me remark—it is unspeakable folly to stereotype religious opinions, as if men were of course to agree in all their views. A young convert just born into the kingdom, wishes to be admitted into the fold of the Good Shepherd. Well, the whole system of religious doctrine is read over. Do you subscribe to this? the whole of this? And then not a step farther may they go, at the peril of heresy. How strange it is that men should imagine that there can be such a thing as for Christians to be just alike in their views of religious truth. They may be alike as far as they go. They may each be correct, while one may be far in advance of his fellow. And as a new truth comes to view, it always sheds its light over all the rest, and modifies the form in which they appear. And while the Spirit continues to throw its light upon the sacred pages, we may expect to modify and enlarge, and in some degree change our view of truth. How absurd to nail down our system and say—There, never change more. I have heard persons reckon it a virtue that they had never changed their views of truth. But I ask, have such persons prayed the prayer of the Psalmist? Have their eyes been opened?

4. The Bible will become to us a new book. Converts say so, and with truth; but it is not true with them alone. Old men, men who have long known God, are made by their experience to say the same thing. A few years since I was laboring in a revival with an elderly minister, a man sixty years old. I shall never forget how that man would say to me time after time, with deep emotion—"I have a new Bible. How striking the promises are. It seems to me as though I had never read them before. So *rich* they are, so full, so precious!" Ah, yes! Nor is this a singular nor an uncommon case. In many, very many instances have persons who have long been

Christians, thus found their Bible a new book, and growing fresh and new as it were every day. It has become so precious, so glorious, so sweet, they could, so to speak, devour it, as the hungry soul devours its needful food. In my own case, let me say, beloved, within the last year the Lord has given to me such views of the Bible, that I have found it difficult to realize that I had ever known before any thing thereof at all. Many a time have I cried out, as the light poured upon the truth—"Lord, I never knew this before,"— and I could scarcely for the time believe that I had ever seen the thing at all. I do not mean I had not, for I know I had before seen great beauties in the Bible, but the light was so great that the spots that before seemed bright, were now hidden in the added splendor, as stars are lost in the light of dawn. Whole trains of passages would crowd through my mind with such glory and freshness—passages which I had preached from again and again, would come in review under a light so new and striking, and with a meaning so full, that it would seem as though I had never known anything of them before, and the thoughts would crowd, and roll, and swell like an infinite tide, till it would appear as if I could preach and preach, and never be done preaching from almost any one of them.

5. Persons will be astonished at their former ignorance of the Bible when God opens their eyes. They will see so much that is new where they thought they knew all before, that they will be forced to exclaim in amazement—how could I have passed these things and not see them. I have read the passages a hundred times, why have I not seen these things before? As if a person should pass through a village in the dark, not knowing it was night, but supposing it was day, and then should go through the same village in actual broad day, and see the houses, and streets, and gardens, and wonder (as he would) why he did not see the village before. Without spiritual light, persons fail to see almost every spiritual truth in the Bible. They are like persons in the dark, while yet they say "We see;"

and when God does indeed open their eyes, and they really see, they are astonished above measure that they had never seen before.

6. Those whose eyes are opened will see a great multitude of things in the Bible which others do not see, and which they will not believe are there, even though you tell them of their existence therein. Read the Bible under the illumination of the Spirit, and you will see myriads of things, which if you tell to others, they will smile at you for a crazy man; they will declare no such things are there, and suspect you to be a little beside yourself. Well let them alone. Let them have their say. They cannot see what you have seen, till they stand in the like strong and clear light. Let two persons pass through a place one in the night, and one in the day, and let the one who passed in the dark think that it was day, and that he saw all that was to be seen. Can he convince him? Wait till he goes through in the day-time, and then talk with him.

And here let me remark, as I said a little ago of the doctrine of Christ's divinity, so it is of the doctrine of Entire Sanctification. Once I could not see that doctrine in the Bible, and now I wonder much why I did not, for now I see it every where, almost. It is true with me as a good sister said of herself—when I first heard of the doctrine of Entire Sanctification, I thought it was no where in the Bible, but now I see that it is *every where*. I can adopt that language myself. It is not strange however, that persons whose eyes are not opened cannot see that doctrine in the Bible. The Bible, much of it, is so written, and perhaps from the necessity of the case, that the soul must be in a certain state, in order to see at all what was in the mind of the Spirit. 'No man can say that Jesus is the Lord but by the Holy Ghost,' says Paul. That is, no man can see Christ as He is—the Lord of our salvation—but by the light of the Holy Spirit spread upon the sacred page. It is curious to see how many notions and conceits men will have of the meaning of the Bible, or how dull of apprehension they will be, and then how clear it will seem when the Lord has opened their eyes. Before, nothing could convince them, now they need nothing to convince them. If a man should pass this meeting-house, supposing he could see when he could not, you could not convince him of its presence; but let his sight be restored or the light shine upon his eyes, and there needs no more—there it stands before his own eyes. The doctrines of Atonement, of Christ's Divinity, of Sanctification—when the light from heaven bursts upon the page, you need no voice to tell you; all silent, you gaze upon the revealed wonders, as when from the deepest midnight the sun breaks from the darkness and the whole landscape lies before you in an ocean of glories. Now Christian friends, I mean what I say; there is a spiritual illumination, a supplying the spiritual eyes with light, in which light the mind sees with a power of demonstration, like that which attends natural vision, the spiritual truths revealed in the Bible. Before this light is supplied, the mind may doubt, and reason, and cavil, and deny; but O, when the sun rises and pours forth its glorious blaze, then everything is revealed, every cavil is hushed, every doubt forgotten, and the soul gazes in silent rapture on the wondrous scene.

7. Our views will become a *wonder* to others, and just in proportion as our eyes are opened. Our views will be reckoned peculiar. Yes indeed, peculiar light will produce peculiar views of course. As far as the Spirit gives us light and we see thereby, our views will be modified, and those who have not the same light, will think them strange, and will wonder at us. How is it, they say, that they find such and such things? We find nothing like that. The Jews think the Christian doctrine blasphemous; they cannot find our Jesus in their Old Testament Messiah. We shall surely be regarded as heretics by those who have not our light. If God gives us light, if the revelations of His word be made to our souls, and especially if we proclaim them to the world, who shall be thought heretics. Let any man push his prayer before God, 'Open Thou mine

eyes that I may behold wondrous things out of Thy law,' and let an answer be granted, and his eyes be really unsealed, and the presbytery will begin to watch him, the whisper will begin to go around, "The brother has a *good spirit,* but his *views* are dangerous"—they must have an eye to him, a committee must be appointed, and they must confer with him to rid him of his strange and peculiar views. What is the matter? Nothing, only the Spirit sheds light upon his mind, and he has got a step or two beyond the stereotype form, that is all. He understands the Bible better than before, has a richer insight into the richness of its promises; the Spirit has anointed him for his work—that is all. And if he ventures to say meekly to his fellow-servants, "Brethren, the Lord hath shown me such things in His word," their counsel will be—our brother seems to have a sweet, heavenly spirit, but his views are peculiar and dangerous, and they must be pronounced heterodox, and he be silenced. This has always been so, and men who are led in advance of their fellow Christians, must be content to be suspected of heresy.

8. Those who are enlightened, will be counted *mystical.* The most spiritual have in all ages been reckoned mystical. There are real mystics to be sure; there are extremes and delusions, and men think they see when they do not; but that does not alter the fact that spiritual men are reckoned mystical by those who are in the dark. Why? Because the former have spiritual eyes, they have spiritual light, and they see and understand things that are entirely invisible, and a complete mystery to others.

9. Those who are enlightened will be considered deranged by those whose eyes are not opened. Christ was thought to be mad. Festus said to Paul, 'Thou art beside thyself, much learning hath made thee *mad,*' you have studied so hard, have gone so deeply into philosophy and theology that you are deranged. Paul indeed answered him most solemnly, 'I am not mad most noble Festus, but speak forth the words of truth

and soberness.' But now wherein lay the difference? Paul had met Jesus by the way and had seen a light from heaven above the brightness of the sun, shining round about him. The light of God had fallen upon him, and now people thought him mad—Festus thought him mad. And why should it not be so? It will be so. It will surely be so. When do we judge a man deranged? Suppose a man's eyes should really be opened as Elisha's were, and those of the young man who was with him, and he should behold the angel of God encamped about him, which is in fact true, or like Stephen's, so that he could look into heaven and see the Son of Man standing at the right hand of God, could behold the realities of the invisible world—would he not be pronounced deranged? Yes indeed. "Put a strait jacket on him—do hear him" they will cry, "he says he sees angels, and chariots, and horses all round him—he sees heaven opened! Blasphemy— away with him—stone him to death!" Why? He tells what he really sees. Let a man but speak out what he sees, and surely he must be deranged. Now men do become deranged—surely they do; they do sometimes become visionary—most certainly; but men's eyes may really be opened too, as Stephen's and Elisha's were, and then others will imagine they are deranged. Those who think so may be honest in their opinion too.

10. Such will almost certainly be persecuted. Why was Paul persecuted? Because his eyes had been opened to see the fullness of the knowledge of Christ Jesus his Lord, and because he was constrained by his love to preach the cross. He had been a persecutor and injurious; he had many friends; but Christ's love had ravished his soul, and he would joyfully pour out his whole being for his Master. And what did he say? Hear him. 'As I came nigh to Damascus, suddenly there shone from heaven a great light round about me, and I heard a voice saying unto me—Saul, Saul, why persecutest thou Me?' and he went on and finished the story of his conversion. They bore impatiently with this, but soon he began again—'while I

prayed in the temple I was in a trance, and saw [the Lord] saying unto me, make haste and get thee out of Jerusalem,' and they could bear it no longer. They gave him audience till this word, and then lifted up their voices and said—'Away with such a fellow from the earth, it is not fit that he should live.' And 'they cried out, and cast off their clothes, and threw dust into the air.' And why? Surely Paul was beside himself, and a horrid blasphemer, and to kill him would be to do God service. They persecuted him. Why? He could see and they were blind. And those who are thus blind often will think that they ought to do many things contrary to those who are spiritual, and whom they regard as dangerous fanatics. I am very far from believing that all persecution arises from mere malicious wickedness. Many in high places and in low, oppose and persecute because they are in the dark, and think they see, and they persecute 'in all good conscience.' They may be, (as indeed they are) wicked for being in the dark, but in the dark, they think their spiritual brethren are mischievous, and must be put down and put out of the church; and think to do God service when they use the exscinding knife. But are they innocent? With all the light around them which God has proffered and now proffers, are they innocent while they remain in the dark? I think not.

11. The illumination of the Spirit will make us *cease* from *man*. We shall cease to expect any such instruction from human lips as shall suffice to qualify us to be useful. Not that God may not use creatures to instruct us in a degree. He does so. But we shall cease to *rest* in them, and we shall go to God feeling entirely sure that from Him alone cometh our help—that He alone can supply the light by which we are to see the things which lie hid in the Word of God.

12. In proportion to the light we enjoy, we shall find ourselves dwelling in the spiritual instead of the natural world. Let a man see as with open vision, the realities which we all believe to exist in the invisible world, let him apprehend them

as we now do the objects of this visible scene, and with which world think you will he be most conversant? With God, heaven, Christ, and the eternal world, or this gross and earthly clod on which we tread? As the mind is opened, it dwells in and communes with the spiritual world, it loses sight of earthly objects—there is a state of mind in which persons can feel the light shining broad and deep upon the soul—God draws near—the soul withdraws from all the outward senses, and retires into its inner sanctuary—God approaches and comes into the inner-most chamber of the mind, and there is silence, far, far from all the world of sense and sight, the soul communes with the eternal God, and if all the world were to throng around and clamor for a hearing, still the soul, withdrawn far within, would heed them not, but in bliss ecstatic drink draughts of ineffable joy from the presence of infinite love, and God be all in all.

I remember well how once I read with astonishment the account of such men as Xavier, where they would have such communion with God as utterly to drive from them all thoughts of earth, and every object of sense. Xavier, you know, on a certain day, was to have a visit from a prince—the viceroy. He went to his chamber, directing his servant to call him at such a time. When the servant entered his room to call him at the hour, there was his master kneeling on the floor, his eyes upturned, and his face shining like that of an angel, wholly insensible to outward things—the servant dared not disturb him. At the end of an hour he came again, still he was so—again, there he knelt. The servant spoke, no answer—he spoke again, no reply—he shook him and succeeded in awakening him from his trance—"Is the viceroy come?" inquired he, 'tell him I have a visit from the King of Kings today, and I cannot leave it"—and he sank back into insensibility, and was shut up in the presence of the Living God. There was a time when I could not understand how Paul could be in such a state of mind, that, speaking as an honest man, he could not tell, as he says, whether in the body or out of the body. But now I can see how he could say so. The mind is so absorbed with spiritual views, as to be insensible to natural objects entirely. The senses are all swallowed up, laid aside. The senses you know are but the organs which the mind uses; but she can do without them; she can retire from the touch, the hearing, the sight, and in the deep sanctuary of the soul sit alone with God. And this occurs when the light of the Spirit shines broadly and fully on the mind. Speak to him he does not hear you—touch him, it does not arouse him—he is gone—gone to the spiritual world; and when he returns and his soul comes back to earth, whether I was in the body I could not tell.

You remember a case among ourselves some years ago. A beloved sister—the Spirit came upon her, and she thought she was in heaven; her heart *was* there, and she thought *she* was there; she forgot she was in the body, the glories of heaven were around her, and she literally leaped for joy. I heard of a case, I think it was in the state of New York. It was that of a deacon. He was sitting in the "deacon's seat," facing the congregation; as the minister was preaching, the Holy Ghost fell upon the deacon. He rose up unwittingly, stretched out his hands upward, his face pale and gazing as it were into heaven, and his countenance radiant as an angel's. The assembly were amazed, the Spirit of God ran like fire through the whole congregation, the arrows of conviction flew like lightening, and the whole body were convulsed with emotion, and many were broken down before the Lord.

13. He whose eyes are opened, will be *solemn*, but it will be a *cheerful* solemnity. It is related of Xavier, that his cheerfulness was so great, that those who were not familiar with him thought him *gay*. David, in his joy, danced with all his might before the ark, when he brought it up from the house of Obed-Edom. There will be nothing like levity, but a deep and solemn cheerfulness, such a cheerfulness as we may suppose

God to possess—a broad, universal smile; the mind smiles in its deepest being; to the very bottom of the heart, there is one deep, broad smile—as God looks forth over His whole creation with a smiling face—the soul is cheerful, peaceful as an *ocean* of peace.

V. *The conditions on which an answer to the request in the text may be expected.*

1. We must *believe* that there are such wondrous things in the Bible, and that God is able and willing to reveal them to us. We must believe in the doctrine of this discourse, to wit, that without divine illumination shed on the Bible by the Spirit, we cannot understand the truths thereof, and that God can so enlighten us as really to make us behold wonderful things, new and before unknown, things hidden from those whom the Spirit does not enlighten, in short, we must believe that the Bible needs to be revealed, that it is not sufficient that these words be written down, and that we read these sentences, but that there must be a personal application and revelation to *us*, by the Spirit, in order to get beyond the letter which killeth, unto the Spirit which giveth life.

2. A sense of our great ignorance, and spiritual blindness. No man will make this petition unless he feels that he is exceedingly blind; unless he realizes that he needs the divine illumination, and how great his darkness is, and his ignorance of the spiritual truths of the gospel, he never will have the enlightening of the Spirit.

3. We must *strongly desire* this divine light. It must be the leading, controlling desire of the mind, our soul must be pressed down with our ignorance, and drawn out in mighty supplications, with strong crying and tears, that God will give us light. The Prophet says, "And ye shall seek me, and find me when ye shall search for me with *all your heart*." There must be such a *longing*, the soul so *set* upon it, as that the soul *cries out* after God. We need to be much in the state of mind in which blind Bartimeus was, that most affecting case, so graphically

described that you seem to see it acted before your eyes. Jesus was passing along with a great multitude around Him, it was all excitement, they came into a village, a blind man sits by the side of the way, where he has often sat before. Bartimeus sits there, as in the East is common to this day—to this day you may see poor creatures blind and lame lying by the way side, half-naked, famishing, dying, and frequently no more notice taken of them than if they were so many beasts—there he sits to beg—he has heard of Jesus of Nazareth, and of his wonderful kindness, and his wonderful cures, and he longs to see Him. Well, Bartimeus hears the noise—he asks, What is it? "Jesus of Nazareth passeth by." He is all on fire—"*Jesus*, JESUS, thou Son of David have mercy on me." "Hush, hush, be still, don't make such an outcry." He cried the louder, "Jesus, Jesus, O Jesus, thou Son of David, have mercy on me." He must be heard, there was a great throng and much noise and he must be heard—he was blind and he must have his sight restored. Jesus could do it and he must gain his ear—he would be heard—when they told him to be quiet he only cried the louder. But Christ heard him. Who is that? A blind man, Lord, nobody but a poor blind beggar. Bring him hither to me. And Bartimeus leaped forth, and they brought him to Jesus. What wilt thou that I should do unto thee? Lord, that I may *receive my sight*. And now mark, see the sweet mercy of the Savior, He restored his sight immediately.

Now you must feel as Bartimeus did, you must have the confidence that he had—for see the confidence Bartimeus had, he believed Jesus *could* heal him, and he wished to afford Him the opportunity. O, if he could but find Him, and when Jesus came that way how he cried out. And so you must feel as to your spiritual sight—that it *must* be obtained.

4. A willingness to encounter all the consequences. Some of the consequences I have told you already. You must be willing to encounter all the consequences, or you cannot be the subjects of the divine illumination.

5. We must *persevere* in faith and asking—for we may not be enlightened at first, any more than the Syrophenician woman was answered at first. Many mistakenly suppose that the very first exercise of faith brings, in their fulness, the blessings promised to faith. But not so. The Syrophenician woman must ask again and again. Jacob wrestled all night with the angel even till break of day. God has his reasons for delay, and they are good ones no doubt, and we should not think the answer will surely come instantly, on the exercise of faith, nor because the answer does not come immediately should we think we do not pray in faith, but we must press our suit, and hold on, and cling to the promises.

6. Right *motives* in asking. Not mere curiosity, but a desire really and truly to glorify God thereby, a desire for the light that we may walk in it, that we may glorify God and hold up the true light in our conduct, by our spirit, our manner, our preaching, our everything. If we have unholy motives in asking it, we shall not obtain the light, we may be well assured.

7. We must *search* the *Scriptures*, if we would expect the light of the Spirit poured upon their pages.

8. We must give up those pursuits, that reading, those objects, which divert our attention, and prevent us from giving our whole souls to the Bible. While our minds are drawn off from the Bible by other things, while we are interested in those authors whose spirit is as directly opposite to that of the Bible as heaven is to hell, how can we hope to have the enlightenment of the Spirit? There is a class of writings, which, in their influence, make the soul totally blind to the glories of the Scriptures—it cannot receive them in such a state of mind. If you give yourself to search for the spirit of Byron, that spirit will come upon you with little effort on your part. It is so congenial to the heart in its selfishness and passion, it will fall upon you without being prayed for. But the Spirit of God will never enlighten you, never. I believe it to be an unalterable condition of communion with the Spirit, that the mind must

be broken off from communion with such corrupt and corrupting authors. You must break loose from them, or you will never enjoy the sweet light of God's Spirit.

9. You must avail yourselves of all the aids within your reach, which will lead you to a right understanding of the Scriptures. I do not mean that a man may not understand the Bible, and have the spiritual illumination in the absence of commentaries and of a knowledge of the original languages; he may get a spiritual acquaintance with the Bible without these, if he give himself thereto with a right spirit, that is, if these helps are out of reach. But if a man can avail himself of the opinions of learned and godly men, he should do so; if he can gain a knowledge of the original tongues, he should do so; if in any other way he can get help from his fellow men, let him do so, remembering meanwhile, that these are by no means indispensable to such a knowledge as is necessary to usefulness and salvation, but very useful in their place, when they can be obtained, and therefore should be used with thanksgiving. If God places you out of reach of all these, then He will enlighten you without their aid, but if they are within your reach, he will not teach you independently of them, those things which are appropriately to be learned from them.

10. It is necessary that we become child-like in our disposition. Now God does not teach, I suppose, by miraculous interposition, properly so called, but when the mind is in a child-like state, the way is open for the Spirit to present the glorious truth, and for the mind naturally to apprehend its deep and transcendent import. The eye then is open, and ready for the light to be shed upon the objects of spiritual vision. But if the mind be committed, if there be a determination to see things just so and no otherwise, we never shall be able to see the truth as it is in Jesus. I pass to make several

REMARKS.

1. I notice the *danger* there is in preaching some of the spiritual truths of the Bible. Not that they tend in themselves to produce mischief, but, men being as they are, those truths will by very many, certainly be perverted. This has always been true, and it is true in respect to many doctrines. Justification by faith—salvation by grace—have they not been sadly perverted? Yet they are most precious doctrines. So the doctrine of spiritual illumination. Many will go straight into delusion under such a discourse as I have preached, or make it the occasion of confirming their minds in a previous delusion. Many will seize hold of some one or other of the consequences I have enumerated of spiritual illumination, and finding such a fact in their own case, they will conclude they are surely divinely enlightened. I said that those who are divinely illuminated will differ much in their views from others, that their views will be reckoned peculiar and wonderful, that they will be thought deranged, that they will be persecuted. Now *we* differ from those about us—we are counted strange and fanatical—they call us crazy or chatter -brained—we are persecuted for our opinions and conduct— therefore we are spiritually enlightened. The doctrines of spiritual religion will certainly be abused—but that is no reason why they should not be preached. They are the food of the saints—the bread of their souls—and shall it be withheld? If others will abuse them, who can help it? They must not be withheld from the true saints who are panting after them, because some will abuse them, and so be lost thereby. It is the less of two evils to preach them for the good of the true saints, though incidental evils result to some, than to withhold them and starve the souls of the faithful and thus curse the world. I have often seen persons confirming themselves in delusion in this way. I know not how many times in reference to this very subject, when I have met with persons laboring under curious delusions, and have expostulated with them, they have quoted my own sermons and writings in support of their fantasies. They will

say, you used to preach that men might be taught of God. Yes, I preach the same doctrine now. But because a man *may* be taught of God, does it follow that you are taught of God in your strange vagaries? Because you may have your eyes opened so as to behold wondrous things out of God's law, is it certain that your wondrous things are contained in the Bible? A certain class of minds will almost surely be deluded, and this most likely to their ruin. To such God says by the prophet, "Behold, all ye that kindle a fire, that compass yourselves about with sparks, walk in the light of your fire, and in the sparks which ye have kindled. This shall ye have of my hand—ye shall lie down in sorrow."

2. Many persons will be led astray in another direction by this subject. Becoming greatly wrought upon, they get a wrong idea, and seek for immense *excitement*. You are to seek with all earnestness, but the thing which you are to seek is not feeling, but light, substantial *light* shed upon the pages of the Bible.

3. Where persons give themselves up to seek states of feeling, and to be carried away by a flood of emotion, it will always react, and create abundant mischief. Men need to be baptized with the Holy Ghost, and if they give themselves to anything else, it may cause much noise and vociferation, but it will never lead them to the state in which they are "light in the Lord."

4. I understand this divine illumination to be a special gift from God—not the gift of miracles—not conversion. The Apostles had it on the day of Pentecost. It is generally included in the Baptism of the Holy Spirit. It is given in different degrees, and at different times. Men need it again and again, and more and more of it. Persons who have been enlightened need still greater illuminations as they go forward.

5. Those whose eyes are not opened are very liable to speak "evil of things which they understand not," and thus wound their own souls and grieve the Spirit of God. It grieves me much to see persons stumbled at things, merely because they

are in advance of their experience. I will mention a case. A man, an elder in the Presbyterian church, who had been such for nearly half a century, and who thought all religious excitement fanaticism, was present at a meeting during a revival in a neighboring church. The Spirit of God came down with power. The elder was much disturbed. At the close, a person in the assembly sank down to the earth, overcome with the power of conviction. The elder cried out angrily, "Get thee behind me Satan." Where is that man now? He opposes everything that is good—all reformations, all progress of good, in a most obstinate and self-willed spirit, and is left apparently to his own destruction. Many do not, I know, go so far as this; but it is astonishing to see how men will speak evil of things which they understand not. It will be well for such to read the solemn words of the Apostle Peter. "These as natural brute beasts, made to be taken and destroyed, speaking evil of the things they understand not, and shall utterly perish in their own corruption, and shall receive the reward of their unrighteousness." It is one of the great dangers to which men are exposed, to oppose, and reject, and speak evil of things simply because the things are beyond their own experience. They seem to think they know all that can be known, and anything else is fanaticism of course. Persons often treat as foolish, and visionary, and childish, and contemptible, the higher states of Christian experience, and only because they themselves have not advanced so far. You should be careful, brethren, lest you speak evil of and reject those very things which you *must* know if you are ever saved.

6. The spiritual members of the Church have always been persecuted by the body of the church. The Bible will tell you so, and all history declares the same thing. The most spiritual ministers and members have always been misunderstood and persecuted by those who are not spiritual.

7. This should not discourage you from seeking spirituality, nor from being spiritual. And, moreover, spiritual persons will

neither be surprised nor offended thereby. They can understand very well why others speak evil and oppose. The spiritual man discerneth all things, but he himself is discerned by no man. The Bible teaches this, and he sees why it is so; he sees why they account him a heretic, and are afraid of him; he sees where they are, but they do not see where he is; he understands their darkness better than they understand his light.

8. The subject accounts for much of the difference of opinion as to the meaning of the Bible. There always will be differences of opinion. It is absurd to think that there can be any system of opinions stereo-typed, and believed alike by the young convert and the adult Christian. What, must men have the full knowledge of the Bible when they are first converted? Are men to make no advances in knowledge of divine things? How are stewards to bring from their treasure things new and old? Then, must nothing *new* be brought forward? O no. You must learn nothing new—must find nothing which is not in the standards. It is to be taken for granted that a thing is wrong of course, if it is not in the standards. It is true, indeed that all will agree in certain doctrines. But it by no means follows that everyone will hold all that is taught in the Bible; neither is it true that men may not be real Christians, and yet be ignorant of many very precious truths taught in the Bible.

9. We all see why so many persons are not deeply interested in the Bible. They have not their eyes opened, have not the divine light shining upon it to make it interesting to them. They are like persons passing a most beautiful region in the dark. They see no beauty, they have no light. Without this light from God, the Bible is a sealed book, and for all spiritual matters of no benefit. And the reading of it for such a purpose, is as dull a work as one can well be engaged in. A man will read his chapter, and five minutes afterwards he knows nothing of what he read. But with the Spirit, the Bible is a world of

wonders; it is a mine of gold, exhaustless; you may dig, and dig, and the deeper you do, only the richer will it become.

10. You may see the reason why ministers, and young men preparing for the ministry are so little interested in making the Bible their study. They lack the divine light that makes it all glorious within, that leads them into the depths of its hidden meaning.

11. Where men possess this divine light, you will never hear them pleading the necessity of reading other books to give the mind proper recreation. If they read other literature at all, it will be not for amusement, but for information. Such a man will not feel bound to read Shakespeare and Scott. He will draw away from them as from an ocean of filth. I may say without extravagance, that to him whose eyes are opened, the Bible will prove a more fertile source of improvement, both moral and intellectual, a more powerful spring of mental action than all other books put together. It opens up a world of thoughts on almost every subject, it starts ten thousand trains; you tread as it were upon enchanted ground, whole masses of thought constantly rising from the bosom of the great ocean of truth; the Psalms, the Prophets, all point you to every part of the universe, the heaven, the earth, and the sea. But without the Spirit, the Bible is bereft of this power.

12. It is true, I believe, that the more of the divine illumination Christians enjoy, the less they read of any thing else than the Bible. Or if they read other things, it is because it will throw light upon, or because the spirit of the works is like the spirit of the blessed Bible. Ask the oldest saint, if he is not tired of his Bible. Tired of my Bible? My Bible? It is more and more my book every year I live. But have you not read it through and through? Yes, but it grows richer and richer every time I go through it. But do you not understand it all? Ah, I learn something continually. I learn more now at a reading than when I first began. Now I know no end to this progression in divine knowledge, for the spiritual mind. The

Spirit keeps bringing up without end, new and more exquisite and glorious displays of the things of God's law. The soul drinks and drinks, and drinks again, and the ocean is never exhausted.

13. Spiritual guides whose eyes are not opened are blind leaders of the blind. I do not mean that a man must have *all* light in order to be a guide at all, a man may guide as far as he knows the way himself, but without enlightenment he can lead but a little way. A vast many ministers are so blind that they can lead but a little way. Many cannot even bring sinners into the kingdom, they have not knowledge enough of the way to carry a sinner into the kingdom and set him down within the gate. Others can take them through the gate, but can guide them little further. Ministers will labor in their way for years and years, and their church will make little progress or none at all. The reason is, their own eyes are not open, and what they do not know they cannot tell to others.

14. You see the importance that ministers shall insist that God shall open their eyes, to enable them to behold wondrous things out of His law. A young man who is *called* to preach, may urge that call before the Lord as a valid reason for the illumination of the Spirit, and he is *bound* to urge his call. O God, hast thou set me a watchman upon Zion's wall, and wilt thou not open my eyes. O, how blind I am! How blind the flock are! How they need enlightenment, my Father open thou mine eyes. A minister ought to press this, and insist on it, and every candidate for the ministry should press it. The Church ought to pray with earnestness that God will open the eyes of their spiritual guides. And every Christian too, ought to pray for enlightenment, that he for himself, may understand the holy word.

15. Many pray to be enlightened who will not fulfill the conditions, who will not give up their own ends, and cast away their prejudices. Of course they remain in the dark.

16. Many mistake and suppose they are enlightened when they are not. They do thus.—They desire a certain thing to be true. They take the Bible and endeavor to make it support their loved doctrine, till at length they seem to see its truth written every where. By long labor the doctrine has become coupled by association with a multitude of passages. Now they are enlightened. O yes, it's as clear as day. No, but they are not enlightened. They are much mistaken. Let me give an illustration, a curious case enough. I received a book, not long since, directed to me with all gravity, as if a revelation from heaven itself. The book is the work of some of the people called Shakers, and it claims to be a revelation from God, to the effect that Christ has come the second time, and that in the person of Ann Lee. In that book a great many passages are adduced to maintain the proposition that Christ's second advent must be in the person of a woman! And all this by the teaching of the divine Spirit! Men think they have the witness of the Holy Ghost to a thing when they have *no* witness of the Holy Ghost to that thing. Bro. Charles Fitch professed to have the witness of the Spirit that the second advent of Christ with the end of the world would occur in 1843. But he was mistaken, as he also is in respects to the doctrine of the annihilation of the wicked. O brethren, do not mistake the persuasions of a heart set in falsehood, nor the vagaries of a fanatical brain for the teachings of the Holy Ghost.

17. Many persons do not care enough about understanding the Bible, to give themselves to pray for the light of the Spirit. They have no *longing* to know what is in the Bible. I know what that indifference is, and I know too what it is to cry out from the bottom of my soul, O God, open my eyes. Listen to the Psalmist. "As the hart panteth after the water brooks so panteth my soul after Thee, O God. My soul *thirsteth* for God, for the living God, when shall I come to appear before God!" Is there any fanaticism there, my brethren? Look at that figure—the poor, tired hart, its tongue out, panting, leaping,

and panting in the desert, and no water. Is there not earnestness there? So interested must you be, your heart panting after God, crying out after Him.

Brethren, there are glorious things in the Bible—wondrous things in God's law—we need the Spirit to open our eyes that we may behold them. To obtain that light we need to pray the prayer of our text—"Open thou mine eyes that I may behold wondrous things out of thy law." Will you give yourselves to pray and seek the Lord, for the light of his Spirit to shine upon the word, to enlighten our eyes, and make us know God's holy truth?

Chapter V.

COMING TO THE WATERS OF LIFE.

Reported by Rev. Henry Cowles. September 2, 1846.

"In the last day, that great day of the feast, Jesus stood and cried, saying, If any man thirst, let him come unto Me, and drink."—John 7: 37.

The feast spoken of here is the feast of tabernacles, of which we have a full account in Leviticus. It was one of the three great feasts observed annually by the Jewish people. Those who are learned in Jewish antiquities give us many interesting and important particulars respecting the mode of celebrating this great festival.

A tabernacle is simply a tent, and the institution might be called *the feast of tents.* Its object was to commemorate the forty years sojourning of the Hebrews in the wilderness when tents were their only dwellings. In observing it, the people gathered the boughs of trees and built themselves booths or tents in the streets or on the house-tops in which they sojourned during the eight days of the celebration.

The last day of the eight was deemed the *great* day, and on this day was observed one ceremony of special interest. Our text evidently alludes to it. The whole people moved in procession to the pool of Siloam and took thence a quantity of water in a golden vessel, carried it thus to the temple, and there poured it out before the Lord. The design of this was to represent the outpouring of the Spirit as taught abundantly by their prophets. It is a most remarkable fact that this great prophecy of the effusion of the Spirit in the times of the Messiah should have been universally understood by the Jews, and that the knowledge of the coming fact should have been kept fresh in their minds, by this ceremony engrafted upon the great festival of tabernacles. Jewish writers concur in stating that the ceremony of bearing and pouring out the water meant just this and was always so understood by the nation.

It was on this occasion that, as stated in our text, Jesus stood and cried, saying "If any man thirst, let him come unto Me and drink." It would seem that He was in the temple as the procession returned from the pool of Siloam, and that He seized upon that solemn, eventful moment to lift up His voice before all the people and call attention to Himself as the great Giver of that very blessing which they were foreshadowing so beautifully in the out-pouring of the waters of Siloam. Then and there did the Man of Sorrows stand out in the presence of the assembled nation and proclaim "If any man thirst, let him—not go to Siloam, but—come unto Me and drink." "He that believeth on Me, as the scripture hath said, out of his belly shall flow rivers of living water." The historian here adds his explanation of these words; "But this spake He of the Spirit which they that believe on Him should receive." Christ very well understood what was represented by the pouring out of the water and He knew that the Jews also understood it; hence His solemn annunciation at this time, calling attention to Himself as the giver of the Holy Spirit according to their well known prophecies. In discussing this subject, I shall show,

I. WHAT IS IMPLIED IN THE TEXT BY THIRST;

II. WHAT IS IMPLIED IN COMING TO CHRIST TO DRINK;

III. WHAT IS THE INVITATION—COME UNTO ME AND DRINK.

1. It is manifest that Christ has no reference to physical thirst for water, but to a state of mind—a state of intense desire, well illustrated by that natural desire for water which is called thirst. No doubt Christ alludes to that intense desire for communion with God which saints often have, and which is aptly expressed by the term, *thirst*.

Thus the Psalmist says—"My soul thirsteth for God, for the living God; when shall I come and appear before God?"

Indeed he often represents himself as thirsting and panting after God—even as the hart pants after the water brooks.

Now whatever the philosophy of the fact may be, every Christian knows it to be a fact that there is such a thing as an intense desire of mind, terminating upon God. The soul feels most intensely that nothing but the smiles and the manifested presence of God can meet and fill its desires.

You know that we are so correlated to the outward world that certain objects awaken intense desires for their attainment. There is that in our physical constitution which creates a demand for its appropriate gratification. A foundation is laid in our constitution for the desire which we call thirst, and the demand is for water.

Now it is very remarkable that there is a state of mind which corresponds to this state of the physical system. There is a thirst of the soul for God. The soul pants and longs after God with a singleness of desire and a burning intensity which nothing can appease but the attainment of its object. As the thirsty man cries out for water and can be relieved by nothing else, so those who are spiritually thirsty cry out after God, and nothing else can by any means suffice to stay their irrepressible longings. When a man is famished with hunger he wants food, and nothing but food will satisfy him; you might spread his table with gold—his soul still cries out for bread; you might clothe his brow with pearls—but you cannot even thus quench his insatiate longings for sustenance: so when the soul thirsts after God, this demand of the inner being can be met only by the actual revelations of God to this mind. God has so correlated our inward being to Himself that the mind struggles and cries out after God and cannot possibly be satisfied with anything else. The words of God are beautiful and lovely in their place—the smiles of His common providence are precious; but the spiritual mind can never be content to take these in place of those inward smiles of Jehovah's presence and those testimonies of His love which He gives to His favored children.

Every Christian knows that the Bible abounds with expression of this intense thirsting after God. And all who have had any experience in the deep things of the divine life in the soul understand well what is meant by this language. It may sound like an unknown tongue to those who have no spiritual discernment. What, they will say—the mind pant after God! What does this mean? Is there really any such thing as this? Yes, I answer, there surely is just such a thing as this—just such a longing of soul for God as the man dying with thirst feels for water. When the inward life is thoroughly developed and the soul renewed into the divine image, it thirsts after God, and longs most intensely for the light of His face.

Now it cannot be doubted that Christ had this very state of mind in His eye, and meant to invite to Himself all those who had this longing after the knowledge and the favor of God. Most perfectly did He understand that it is not naturally possible for us to attain the highest state of blessedness on earth unless we draw and drink the living waters of life which He has promised, and which He alone can give.

I have said that this spiritual thirst is a certain state of mind. It may be defined thus—an intense desire for the fulness of a present salvation—a desire to realize in our own case what it is to be filled with all the fulness of God. In this state the mind pants after the fulness of a present enjoyment of God. This is the state which Christ had under His eye; a state in which the soul longs and pants after the fulness of a present communion with God.

The state ultimately desired by the individual who thus longs after God may be expressed thus; a universal and entire cleansing of the mind from all that pollutes—in which all wanderings of thought in prayer are suppressed and controlled:—the appetites are brought into subjection and kept there;

and soul lives and moves and has its being as it were in an atmosphere of God and of purity.

This state of mind is well illustrated in the experience of a lady, a letter from whom I saw some years since in R———. A friend of mine there showed me a letter written many years since by his grandmother. In this she gives in detail the course of her experience, showing how her mind had been greatly stirred up on respect to her falling so often and so sadly into bondage to sin—in respect to wanderings of thought in prayer and those various things over which Christians so often mourn. She felt the bitterness of these things, and came to feel at length that she could not live in such a state of bondage any longer.

In reading the scriptures, moreover, she had noticed that the Apostles got above this state of mind and evidently lived in liberty and not in bondage. Pursuing this train of inquiry she lighted upon many of those promises in the Bible which may well be called "exceeding great and precious," and she believed them. She knew they were the word of the Lord, and she had long since settled it in her mind that God must be believed in all He said. Of course her next step was to take hold of these promises and cry to God in mighty prayer that He would fulfill them in her case. She did so. Her feelings became so intense that the strongest language of scripture expressive of thirsting, longing, panting after God, was none too strong to express her actual state of mind. So earnestly did her soul agonize for this blessing that she literally cried aloud after God, saying, "'I cannot let Thee go unless Thou bless me'—I must absolutely die in this room if Thou give me not this blessing which I so greatly need. O, she cried, I cannot live without it."

Now she came to realize that very state of mind of which the sacred writers spake. She knew what it is to have the soul thirst and long after God, yea, the living God. She thirsted for that water of life which Jesus had promised, and she rushed to His feet to lay hold there of a present salvation from sin. I need not say that such seeking is never in vain. Jesus Christ has said, "If any man thirst, let him come unto Me and *drink*." "He that believeth on Me, out of his belly shall flow rivers of living water." Such was the experience of this lady.

This hungering implies a right state of the will. The hungering itself is a state of the sensibility inasmuch as it is simply desire and feeling; but it results from the heart's being in a right state, and could not exist if the heart were in a wrong state. The thirst for spiritual blessings does not, as some seem to suppose, imply that the individual is in a sinful state, but that he is in a holy state comparatively;—yet is he striving to get higher and still nearer to God.

Again, this thirsting implies a self-loathing and disgust towards everything that stands in the way of the most intimate communion with God. Men find that the outward life is not so crucified but that it seems to come between the soul and God. There is something that prevents the soul from entering into that great, deep, calm communion with God, and the mind is in agony because it finds itself thus withheld from God. There is a waywardness of the physical propensities—an agitation and fluttering which I hardly know how to describe, but which most Christians understand but too well in their own experience; and when this develops itself, it comes directly in the way of entering into real and deep peace with God. It creates a sort of effervescing and agitation, not itself sinful perhaps, but excessively annoying and dangerous inasmuch as it often operates powerfully as temptation to sin. Many of you doubtless know what this is, and you also know perhaps how the soul is thrown into deep agony by means of this conflict with the flesh, and gives itself up to mighty energizings of prayer and faith that it may be delivered from this foe within and brought into a state of pure and perfect peace. This is one of the forms of thirsting for the waters of life.

Again, this thirst implies a great drawing of the Spirit of God. The soul is drawn out after God with a deep and powerful drawing, so that it truly yearns after God, and feels that nothing can begin to satisfy this craving desire of the soul with its Maker. It deserves special notice here that this often seems to the individual himself to be the very calling of the Spirit of God, as if he heard that voice and was conscious of being drawn upward towards the blessed God by some influence not self-originated. The spiritual christian recognizes this call at once as the voice of his Beloved.

Again, this thirsting for the water of life implies being heartily sick of sin and heartily sick of tampering with anything that can become an occasion of sin and that embarrasses the soul and hinders its living in the closest communion with God. It implies a supreme desire to live wholly for God and an utter loathing of any form of life which falls short of this. How often in looking at this point have I thought of Paul's experience. "I am crucified with Christ; nevertheless I live: yet not I, but Christ liveth in me; and the life which I now life in the flesh, I live by the faith of the Son of God who loved me and gave Himself for me." The Apostle here develops a state of mind which I fear but few enter into and thoroughly understand. I live, he says, yet not I; not I, the same Paul or Saul who once followed the flesh and lived afar from God—it is not the same I, that now lives, but it is Christ within me that now becomes my life. He knew what it was to have a new and spiritual life energizing through all his inmost soul.

Beloved, how many of you know what this means? Who of you have tasted in your own experience and know the blessedness of this divine life?

II. We are to enquire *what is implied in coming to Christ to drink.*

1. A belief in His real divinity; a belief that Christ is truly God. This cannot fail to be obvious to you upon a due examination of the text in its connection. For, what is the thing about which the Savior is here speaking? Nothing else surely but the gift of the Holy Ghost; and since the Holy

Ghost is also divine—nothing else but the gift of God himself to the soul. The historian himself explains our Savior's language;—"this spake He of the Spirit which they that believe on Him should receive."

Coming to Christ then, according to this invitation is coming to one who can give God to the soul. Of course therefore none can come in faith unless he has confidence in the true divinity of the Lord Jesus Christ.

Take another view of this. The object of this thirst of the soul is nothing other than God Himself. The soul as I have already said, when thirsting in the sense of the text, thirsts after God—after His presence—His love and His communion. Now then, while thirsting after God, can we come to Jesus to receive the blessing unless we believe Him to be truly divine? Can any being who is less than divine give us communion and peace with God? Can one who is not God Himself give God to our souls?

Again, mark the language of the text—"Come unto Me and drink." If any man thirst truly after God, let him come unto *Me*—I can quench his thirst, and supply all his wants. How can we believe this unless we truly believe that Christ is God?

There is no escape from this course of argument. Some may seek to escape by maintaining that the thirst spoken of is not really a thirst after God. But surely every spiritual Christian knows that this is nothing else than a longing after God. What else is it? Does the soul thirst after a mortal man, or after an angel? Is it the favor of man or angel which awakens such intense desires and irrepressible thirstings? Nay verily; the Christian does not thus learn Christ. God and God alone is the supreme object of his thirst, and he comes to Jesus to be filled with God. How can he intelligently do this, unless he believes in His real divinity?

Again, this coming to Christ implies *self-renunciation*. None will ever come so long as they can find enough of good in themselves and without Christ to satisfy the demands of their own mind. This is most obvious. Their own vessel must be empty before they can rationally come to Christ to have it filled. None will ever come to Christ for these waters of life so long as he supposes he can get them by any efforts of his own. One's own righteousness must be utterly renounced and all one's own ways of being saved; else there will be no real coming to trust in Christ. Self must be utterly renounced.

Again, coming to Christ implies a reception of Him by faith as the promised Messiah, as our own Savior, Redeemer, and Mediator before God. There must be a personal appropriation of Christ by faith to one's self as ours in all those respects in which the divine gospel plan makes Him the Savior of lost men.

All this implies that the Spirit takes the things of Christ and shows them to us. We have no reason to suppose that any soul ever receives Christ as his own Savior except as the Spirit sets before that mind just views of its own need and of the perfect adaptation of Christ to supply that need.

Again, this coming to Christ implies some degree of expectation of receiving the blessing to be sought. It is naturally impossible to come to Christ without faith in His promises; and this faith you will readily see must imply some degree of expectation that if we come as we are invited to do, we shall receive.

III. *What does this invitation imply?*

As I have already said, it implies His divinity. On this I need not now enlarge.

Of course the invitation implies His entire ability to give the blessings needed. If He be really divine, none need to doubt His ability. If He promises to give, we ought not to doubt that He can.

Again, the invitation implies also His willingness to bestow upon us the spiritual good promised. The very promise itself most perfectly implies this.

The promise implies also that if we do come to Him to drink, we shall receive. When He invites, it is not to tantalize; it is not to raise expectation only to disappoint it again; it is not that He may send us away empty and confounded; no, but it is to induce us to come and enjoy the bliss of being blessed; and this of course implies the strongest, richest pledge that if we do come in honesty of heart and in humble faith we shall receive the promised blessings.

Again, we must get this blessing of Christ and of no one else. He doubtless intended to teach this most emphatically, that if anyone thirsted for the waters of life, that soul must come unto Him and to none other but to Him for those waters.

Mark how beautifully and impressively He taught this. See Him in front of that lofty temple and in the presence of that vast triumphant procession as they move slowly along. He waits till the priest has brought forward the golden vessel of water from Siloam's pool and poured it forth at the foot of the altar, He stands by in silence till the ceremony is completed, and then He lifts up His voice before the assembled nation and cries aloud, Ho, ho, all ye people of Israel, ho, all ye children of the promises and covenants of the Lord, "If any man thirst, let him come unto Me and drink." With Me are the waters of real life. "He that believeth on Me, as the scripture hath said, out of his belly shall flow rivers of living water."

What an announcement is this! And with what mingled emotions was it received by those dense masses of human beings on whose ears it fell! Some of the Pharisees were mad enough to murder Him on the very pavements of the temple; they would not have scrupled to shed His blood, so enraged were they at Him—but He meekly goes on in His Master's work, and perhaps through fear of the people they did not dare just now to lay their hands upon Him. "Many of the people, it is beautifully added, "when they heard this saying, said, Of a truth this is a Prophet." Some said one thing and some another, so there was a division among them. What a scene of prodigious excitement did this startling announcement make! Such a sort of excitement the gospel in these later days often produces where it is announced with demonstration of the Spirit and the power of God.

REMARKS.

1. Many persons have none of this thirst, for several reasons.

(1.) They have never suffered themselves to be thoroughly convinced of sin. I say, never *suffered themselves,* for mark me, they could not fail of being thus convinced if they would not resist the Holy Ghost. His Spirit would reprove them of their sin if they would not resist His reproof. But they do resist, and hence they never know the depth of their own guilt and vileness so as to be led to cry out after deliverance and to thirst after God.

(2.) Many know not this thirst and supply, because though they have had a conviction of sin, yet they have never believed and tasted so as to know the blessedness of receiving these waters of life. In fact men need to know God by having some degree of communion with Him before they will have their desires kindled intensely for more and deeper communion. The heart must first be submitted to God, and some experience be had of the rich blessedness of gospel peace and gospel love; than the soul will naturally thirst after God. But multitudes never have this thirst because they have not tasted of these waters.

(3.) I am often struck with the fact that many seem to know nothing of the meaning of such language as the Bible employs to express the longings of the soul after spiritual blessings. They confess that when they read such passages as the text, and many passages to which I have alluded in the Psalms of David, they really know nothing of this thirsting: these terms would express a far stronger desire than they have ever felt. It is astonishing to see how many there are who never know God—never have the soul cry out after a full and perfect salvation—never feel a longing, a quenchless, burning desire, just like a natural thirst, which nothing else can supply but the very thing desired. They do not understand how the mind gravitates towards God. They do not know what it is to have God become the natural food and drink of the soul, so that nothing but God Himself can satisfy its demands. There is such a state in which nothing but God can satisfy the demands of the soul. If all the angels of heaven were given us it would not satisfy; if everything else besides God in the whole universe were laid at our feet, it would not suffice; it would not be *the thing* which the soul craves. This object of supreme desire is nothing else but God. O how the soul cries out after God, the infinite God, the perfect, the glorious, the ever-blessed God! There is a most beautiful and wonderful correlation established between God and the human soul which lays a foundation for this want, this demand of the soul for God as its only satisfying portion. Consequently when the soul comes into an upright state, and the inner voice of its spiritual nature is heard, that voice cries out after God and feels that the soul must live in God and that to depart from God is hell itself. The living in and with God and being sunk in Him, is the natural, the necessary and the eternal good of the soul.

In view of this great and glorious good, where and what is all that pertains to this outward life? It effervesces for a day—it bustles for a moment;—it is, and then it is no more; men may be fascinated by it for an hour: but when the soul comes to understand God, then nothing but God can suffice. Nothing else can meet its demands.

It is remarkable that this is the sum of all the blessings promised to the saints of God in the Bible. To Abraham God said—"Fear not—I am thy shield and thy exceeding great reward." Mark this language. God does not say—I will give thee an exceeding great reward—but I am—I Myself am thy glorious reward. I give you Myself as thy portion.

So God often represents Himself as being the infinite good of the soul. The spiritual Christian can easily understand this.

On the other hand, some think of heaven as being some place which is itself blessed. They fancy its streets to be of gold—its rivers and flowers and fruits combine every thing that can regale the senses and charm the taste, and the place itself becomes in their view the heaven, and would be if there were no God there.

But all such views are false and delusive. Really it is the presence of God and nothing else that makes heaven blessed. There the mind is swallowed up and forever enfolded in God. There the glorious God becomes truly the portion and the everlasting blessedness of every holy soul.

(4.) Many confound conviction of sin with this thirst for the waters of life. A state of conviction will truly precede it; but this thirst is entirely a different thing, and arises from the fact that the mind really knows and has entered into the enjoyment of God. You recollect how our Lord most beautifully represents His people as eating His flesh and drinking His blood. Now this must certainly denote a cordial reception of Christ by a living faith. And the previous hunger and thirst which are always implied in eating and drinking must in their spiritual acts imply much more than simply conviction of sin.

(5.) Many have not this thirst because they allow themselves to thirst for other things. The two are absolutely incompatible with each other. There is even among professors of religion a vast deal of thirsting after the outward life and its enjoyments. When this is indulged the inward thirst after God must cease.

2. It is a great blessing to have this inward thirst developed.

It is in itself a very great blessing to have the soul thus drawn out after God. The very desire is a heavenly state of mind, for you are conscious that your exercises are perfectly reasonable and that your affections are now taking hold of objects which are most perfectly worthy of an immortal mind.

And if the state of desire is blessed, how much more so is the fulfillment of it? O, to be filled even on earth with all the fullness of God! This is of all things below, most blissful!

3. When this has ceased in the mind, one can have no reason to hope that he is going to heaven. If the mind has become so apostate from God, there is no hope left. Why should God take that soul to heaven which has no longings for His presence?

4. Many persons stop short with this thirst because they have not faith to come to Christ. Do you see them come to Christ and plead—"Lord, didst not Thou say—if any man thirst, let him come unto Me and drink, and now, Lord, I have come, expecting Thou wilt give me those blessed waters." Do you see this state of mind? No. They do not come to Christ believing absolutely that He will give them the blessings they need.

I can well recollect a scene in my own experience which is in point here. My soul was drawn out exceedingly for this blessing and I did not see why I did not attain it. My heart seemed full of prayer, echoing and echoing with pleadings and promises, till all at once the thought came across my mind—you do not believe you shall receive. I instantly thought of a dear friend of mind who would always anticipate my wants, who seemed to have the faculty always of foreseeing the things I needed, and who would be sure to supply them as if this was the chief pleasure of his existence. Then I asked myself—Do you as much expect Christ to supply your wants as you expect it of this earthly friend? I saw then that I did not. I saw the shameful unbelief of my state of mind, and I felt so rebuked and so perfectly ashamed that I could not help crying out—"O my blessed Jesus, I have not had so much faith and confidence in Thee as I have often had in a man!"

So, many are withered and blighted because you do not believe that God is drawing, but you are resisting. O, you do not believe. Jesus Himself comes near—yea very near;—He puts the cup into your very hand and says "drink, yea drink abundantly, O beloved;" but alas, how many still will not believe.

O this fountain of life—what is it but the fountain of God bubbling up in your inward, spiritual being. Verily the blessing offered you is nothing less than the glorious God Himself; and now will you not believe? If any man will come believing, the voice divine says, I will give him of the waters of life freely.

Chapter VI.

ON DIVINE MANIFESTATIONS.
Reported by Rev. Henry Cowles. March 18, 1846.

"If ye love me, keep my commandments; And I will pray the Father, and he shall give you another Comforter, that he may abide with you for ever; Even the Spirit of truth, whom the world cannot receive, because it seeth him not, neither knoweth him: but ye know him; for he dwelleth with you, and shall be in you. He that hath my commandments, and keepeth them, he it is that loveth me; and he that loveth me shall be loved of my Father, and I will love him, and will manifest myself to him. Judas saith unto him, (not Iscariot,) Lord, how is it that thou wilt manifest thyself unto us, and not unto the world? Jesus answered and said unto him, If a man love me, he will keep my words: and my Father will love him, and we will come unto him, and make our abode with him."

John 14: 15-17; 21-23.

"Wherefore come out from among them, and be ye separate, saith the Lord, and touch not the unclean thing: and I will receive you, And will be a Father unto you, and ye shall be my sons and daughters, saith the Lord Almighty. Having therefore these promises, dearly beloved, let us cleanse ourselves from all filthiness of the flesh and spirit, perfecting holiness in the fear of God."

2 Cor. 6: 17, 18, and 7: 1.

In remarking upon these verses it is not my design to dwell upon all the thoughts they present or might suggest. I shall aim to illustrate,

I. The conditions of acceptance with God as here developed.
II. The conditions of hearty obedience to God.
III. The conditions of Divine manifestations.
IV. What is implied in these manifestations.

I. The conditions of acceptance with God.

This topic has been recently dwelt upon at considerable length in your hearing, and it has been shown most conclusively that the once unalterable condition of acceptance with God is entire obedience to his law. You must fully set your heart to obey God in all things—at all times—under all circumstances—you must in fact obey the whole law of God in spirit; that is—it must be the supreme, fixed, strong purpose of your soul to do all the will of God.

This is undoubtedly assumed in our texts, especially in the one from 2 Corinthians. In the context the Apostle urges the church at Corinth not to connect themselves unequally with unbelievers, urging as a reason that sin can have no fellowship with holiness; the temple of God no agreement with idols; "for ye," said he, "are the temple of the living God, for God has promised to dwell and walk in you;" and the condition of this promise is that you come out from among them and be separate, and touch not the unclean thing; then God will receive you, and will be a father unto you and ye his sons and daughters. Dropping the borrowed language of the Old Testament, the Apostle goes on to give in his own language what he understands to be the import of these promises and of their conditions. "Having therefore these promises, dearly beloved, let us cleanse ourselves from all filthiness of the flesh and of the spirit, perfecting holiness in the fear of God." These therefore are the conditions of God's dwelling in us—cleansing ourselves from all filthiness—perfecting holiness in the fear of God. Becoming pure in heart and life—renouncing all filthiness of either the flesh or the spirit;—this and nothing less than this can be the condition of acceptance with God.

This same truth is also plainly implied and taught in the passage from John's gospel. "If ye love me, keep my commandments. Then will I pray the Father and he will give you the Comforter &c." So again, "He that hath my commandments and keepeth them, he it is that loveth me, and he that loveth me, shall be loved of my Father, and I will love him and will manifest myself unto him." Obedience and love, evermore inseparable, are here made the condition of the divine favor.

So every where throughout the Bible we are taught that God accepts only those who fully and most heartily obey him.

Indeed it cannot possibly be otherwise. The nature of God forbids that it should be. What! God accept a rebellious spirit and own him as his child! God smile on a heart still sinning! This were to subvert his throne, and abolish all moral distinctions in his kingdom! This were to treat sin and holiness alike, and show that he regards neither! This is just as impossible as for God to cease to be holy!

It must be therefore that God makes sincere and full-hearted obedience the one unalterable condition of his favor. It would be infinitely dishonorable to him to accept anything less.

The same truth is implied in making repentance a condition of being accepted of God. For repentance is nothing else than a hearty turning away from all sin to the full-hearted love and service of God.

II. We must next inquire for *the conditions of rendering this obedience.*

Full obedience, we have seen, is the condition of God's favor; but we have still to look for the conditions of this obedience itself. How shall we obey? Under what influence and motives and efforts may we hope to yield this obedience?

1. *Faith.* It has often struck my mind forcibly in reading the seventh and eighth chapters of Romans that the Apostle is here illustrating the impossibility of obeying the law of God without faith in Christ; not the impossibility of obeying it at all; but of obeying it under *legal motives.* Hence he shows that the law when it comes in contact with a depraved heart, the cross not being present, only provokes resistance and stirs up the depths of the heart's depravity. And the utmost that can be effected is to elicit ineffectual struggles between the reason and conscience on the one hand, and imperious lusts on the other. But faith coming in gives the victory.

Such is manifestly the strain of his illustration in these chapters.

Again in Hebrews 11:6, we read that without faith it is impossible to please God. This is a most concise and explicit assertion to our point.

Galatians 5:6 teaches that "in Christ Jesus neither circumcision nor uncircumcision avails any thing; but faith (alone avails) which works by love." That faith which becomes efficient through love is the capital thing in the gospel scheme. This avails; nothing else does or can.

In Acts 5:9 we have a passage strikingly in point. Peter is there testifying before the great council at Jerusalem, as to the manner in which the Gentile converts were sanctified. He says, God gave them the Holy Ghost even as he did us, and "put no difference between them and us, *purifying their hearts by faith.*" By faith then did they come into a state of purity of heart and thus sincerely and fully obey God.

To the same purport is Acts 26:18 where the Lord appears to Paul and commissions him to go to the Gentiles and "open their eyes . . that they may receive forgiveness of sins and inheritance among them that are sanctified—(how?) *by faith* that is in me." On this point then we see that the testimony of scripture is ample and explicit.

III. We are next to notice *the conditions on which God and Christ will manifest themselves unto the soul.*

This is expressly stated in the passage taken from the gospel of John. The entire scope of this passage is worthy of consideration. Christ was about to leave his disciples by his own death and ascension to heaven. Yet he bids his disciples not to grieve—tells them that he will come again,—yea come himself, with the Father, and take up his abode with them. The world, says he, shall not see me in these visitations and indwelling of my presence with you, but ye shall see me. How, asks Thomas, how can this be that thou wilt show thyself unto us, and yet the world shall not see thee? Then comes the explanatory answer. "If a man love me, he will keep my words and my Father will love him and we will come unto him and make our abode with him." Love, therefore, leading the Christian to keep Christ's words—that is, love prompting and securing full obedience—these are the conditions, as here revealed.

So elsewhere throughout the Scriptures. So in our passage from Corinthians. "Come out from among them and be ye separate, saith the Lord, and I will receive you." "Let us cleanse ourselves from all filthiness of the flesh and of the spirit, perfecting holiness in the fear of God;" so shall we realize the fulfillment of those exceeding great and precious promises which pledge us the indwelling presence and manifestations of God.

I have shown that according to the scriptures, faith is the condition of real and full obedience. Of course faith is also a condition of these manifestations. The soul must first believe in Christ and take hold of divine strength for its aid and of divine truth with realizing apprehension, before it will be thoroughly obedient.

Now considering faith as one of the conditions of these divine manifestations, the question may be asked—Must our faith fasten specifically on these promises of manifestations and plead with confidence for this particular blessing before it can be received? This is an interesting and important question.

In answer to it I remark, that this form of faith is not particularly alluded to among the conditions given in either of our texts. Obedience and love—purity of heart and life—are the things there specified.

Yet the general law in the spiritual world is clear and decisive on this point. When God gives a particular promise like this of manifesting himself to his people, he requires specific faith in that promise—a definite laying hold of those very words or at least of the idea of that promise, and a pleading of the faithfulness of God for its fulfillment.

Famine rages in Israel. Drought has parched all the land. The Lord is about to send rain, and to send it in answer to prayer. Yet he simply tells Elijah to go and meet Ahab. Elijah obeys. But we well understand that rain does not come without special prayer. In due season he bows his soul with mighty energy for rain.

There are passages of scripture which plainly show that specific blessings being promised, specific faith must take hold of these promises as a condition of their being given. In Ezekiel 36: 37, the Lord having promised to cleanse his people and give them a new heart, declares explicitly—"I will yet for this be inquired of by the house of Israel to do it for them." This is given here as a universal principle of the government of God. So far as we know, the Lord never departs from this principle in his spiritual administration towards his people. Whenever he has promised a blessing either to his church or to individuals, the mere promise does not secure the bestowment; faith must take hold of that promise; you must ask, and ask believing that plighted word of the Lord;—then he gives it and not before. Thus God elicits prayer—makes us prize the blessing and love the Giver.

The conditions then, briefly, of these manifestations are;—full-hearted obedience to all known duty—walking in faith, love and obedience; and taking hold by faith of God's promise for this very blessing. Take hold of this promise and wait earnestly and in confidence, honestly and earnestly meeting every revealed condition. Then shall the blessing be given.

IV. *What is implied in Christ's manifesting himself to his people?*

It would seem that it must mean something more than is commonly meant by faith; for the word *manifest* refers our minds rather to *sight* than to faith. I will do more, Christ seems to say, than make you believe; I will make you see. Your apprehensions of God and of his Son shall be most vivid. It shall be as if you *saw* with open vision. This shall be more than mere faith.

It is also something more than love—at least more than such love as is implied in keeping God's commandments; for so much as this is a condition of these manifestations; hence must precede them; and therefore cannot be the blessing itself.

We have a clue to the real meaning in the paraphrase which our Lord himself gives. "My Father will love him, and we will come unto him and make our abode with him." O there must be precious meaning in such words as these. "We will come unto him"—the Father and the Son will come to visit him and reveal themselves to his soul—and this for no transient hour; but "we will take up our abode with him." This must be very like heaven! What more, we might almost ask, would be requisite to make one's bliss like heaven?

What then, ask we again, is implied in these promised manifestations? More of course than giving a man the Bible—and more than making a man understand the Bible. These gifts, great though they be, are never designated in such language as we find in the text. Positively:

(1.) These manifestations imply, *the baptism of the Spirit*. The context plainly shows that Christ had this in his mind. After giving the promise as in our text, He proceeds to promise the Comforter, to show that he would teach all things and bring those things to their remembrance which Christ had said to them. He would "glorify Christ, for he would receive of Christ's and show it unto them."

(2.) The text shows that the blessing promised, means the indwelling of the Father and of the Son by the Spirit. And this, as I have said is declared to be not a visit merely, but taking up an abode—not as a way-faring man who tarries for a night, but as a resident who makes your house his home.

Let it not be supposed from what I have said that the child of God to whom these manifestations are made, and who received the special baptisms of the Spirit, has of course never had the Spirit before. Let no one imagine that the faith and love and obedience which as I have said must precede these manifestations as their condition, can ever exist without the Spirit. By no means. But there is a higher kind and measure of the Spirit's influence and also a lower. The latter is essential to any sincere faith and love; the former comes only in those glorious manifestations of which our Lord here speaks.

This higher influence is said in our context to be sent by the ascended Savior on those who truly love him and fully keep all his commandments. The disciples plainly had received a lower measure of the Spirit's influence before;— now they receive a higher measure in the baptism of the Spirit.

(3.) Another thing is implied in these manifestations. Christ will actually reveal himself to the mind so that it shall know him in his official character and relations. And there is a deep and precious meaning in this. Often have I been struck with this in my own experience. Some new aspect of the Savior's character, or some new point in his relations comes before my mind with great vividness; I wonder I had not seen this before; I seem not to have been aware that Christ sustained this relation, and I now embrace him in this new relation and rejoice that I find him meeting and supplying one more want of my soul.

Thus for example, when Christ revealed a new feature of his relations to me through these words—"Thou shalt call his name *Jesus; for he shall save his people from their sins.*" Then I saw him not merely an atoning Redeemer, but a Sanctifer—one who came to save his people from sinning. Then my soul knew Christ in this other and more glorious relation. But more of this.

(4.) When Christ manifests himself to the soul, the Christian is rather a *knower* than a *believer.* He does indeed believe—but he also more than believes. He not merely believes that Christ died and made atonement, but he is made to know Christ. How natural is the language which a Christian enjoying these manifestations uses so spontaneously —"I believed before, but now I *know* it." I was often struck with the strong language of Elder Marks on his sick and dying bed. He did not say—"I believe," but "I *know*." He would sit in his great chair, when he could not lie down, and laugh and then cry, overcome and convulsed often with deep, unutterable emotions because God was showing him his own blessed truth so that he *knew* it.

Now in such cases, this strong perception which we call seeing and knowing is not of the body but of the mind. It is not your external eye that sees, but your internal eye. Hence your perceptions are so clear and so vivid.

We here observe that when Christ manifests himself, there is something more than mere belief. There must be belief before this; a belief that begets love and obedience; but when Christ manifests himself by his Spirit, there is something more than this, Christ says, "the world shall not see me, but ye shall see me." Did he mean that he would come again during their life-time in his body, and that they should see this? No; but that he would make such revelations of himself that they should know that they had a personal interview with their Lord. He told them he was going away to heaven, but they need not grieve, for he should return again and show himself.

Now did all this mean only that they should have faith in him? Much more than this;—it meant that he would return and show himself and they should know assuredly that Christ was with them.

Again, when Christ manifests himself to the soul, it must be that the mind in some way has an assurance that it is not deceived, and that the manifestation is actual.

I have spoken of personal interviews with Christ. You are aware that in various ages there have been many saints who have asserted that they had interviews with Christ. There were many cases of this before Christ's incarnation. Christ manifested his glory to Moses; to Isaiah—to John in Patmos—to Paul as he himself assures us. And in every age since, there have been those who have supposed themselves to have interviews with Christ. They are wont to say—"I have seen him." I have heard a man in this place say, he had seen Christ. He could not rid himself of the impression that he had truly seen the Lord.

Now on this point I am not going to say that Christ manifests himself to the bodily eyes of the saints, but the revelation is such that they do not know but they see him with their eyes. Perhaps it seems to them altogether as if they did.

I have often in your presence alluded to the circumstances attending my own conversion. When Christ first revealed himself to me, I certainly seemed to see him, and to rush and fall at his feet as really as if I were to turn about now and fall at Br. Mahan's feet. I felt a powerful drawing of soul towards him, as if my very soul would be drawn out of me;—I rushed into a private room and there I seemed to meet him. There—so it seemed—was Jesus—the very Savior!

Now this I do not mention because it is a peculiar case; it occurs or has occurred somewhat frequently in the experience of the people of God. Christians have often felt that they have seen Christ. They have no more question about the fact than about any other. They do not know that they see him with the bodily eye, but their *mind* sees Christ, and it makes all the impression on the mind of seeing.

Christ does not *usually* manifest himself so that one sees a form and shape; but so that the soul is perfectly conscious of the presence of Christ. I know a minister who has told me that at one particular period of his life it was frequently just as real to him that Christ was with him as that any man ever was. It seemed to him a matter of consciousness that Christ was present as much as it ever was that another man is present;—as much as if Christ had actually come down from heaven and kept by his side daily. This is Christ's making himself manifest.

It is intimated also that the Father comes and takes up his abode in the soul. This implies that the Holy Ghost reveals both Christ and the Father. Now it is certainly remarkable that in all Christian experience there is such a distinction between the Father and the Son. The Father is revealed as a father; Christ as Savior and Redeemer. The soul seems to know God distinctly in these two relations. It has no misgivings in respect to God's being indeed a father, more than any child has respecting his own earthly father. So also the soul regards Christ as really the Redeemer, and comes to him as such.

Another thing. These manifestations involve the establishment of the soul's love and confidence. This is no doubt one of the principal designed objects of those manifestations. In the case of the primitive disciples, Christ meant to give them such a hold of the gospel as should prepare them for coming trials;—and should make them *knowers* and not mere believers.

Another result. Whenever Christ is thus manifested the external evidences of revealed religion have no longer any special force on the mind, comparatively; the minds' reliance is hence-forward chiefly on the internal evidence. I have often thought that if Christ had not revealed himself to me so that my mind took hold powerfully of the internal evidence, and was impressed forcibly by the manifestations to which I have alluded, I should have been an infidel, and should have apostatized utterly. It has often seemed that my natural incredulity is so great that nothing else but this could have kept me from being an infidel. My mind was in the habit of constant agitation under the questions—How do I know that this is so? How do I know but all this is delusion? Satan would often present these difficulties in the strongest light. I would set myself to reason upon them, and could see that according to all the rules of logic, all is clear and certain; yet at the same time I was conscious of such a state of mind that I knew I should not have believed if Christ had not given me conscious and certain manifestations.

These manifestations greatly confirm the mind in its convictions. Religion becomes a matter of experience so that the soul cannot but believe. If Christ manifests himself to the soul once, it can doubt no more. Yet such manifestations may be frequent, and if the conditions are fulfilled, will be.

Light from the scriptures is another result. The promise as applied to us, is that the Spirit shall take of the scriptures and show to us. Persons thus enlightened and privileged see more of the Bible than ever before. They have a new kind of confidence in it. They take up their Bible and find there new things unseen before.

RESULTS.

1. Many professors of religion seem to have lost sight of this truth. It is remarkable to see to what an extent this is true. Perhaps they have lost sight of the strong faith which must precede them; perhaps they conceive of nothing better in religion than a dim hope, and enjoy nothing more. They seem to forget the conditions—"If a man love me, he will keep my sayings, and my Father will love him." In fact some seem to have lost the whole subject.

Again, there are not a few who understand this subject—know that they may have such manifestations; but have got the idea that it means more than it does; or their notions of what it is are entirely vague; they call it perhaps assurance of faith, or assurance of hope; but they fail of attaining because they quite overlook the conditions, or seem to forget that there are any conditions at all. Or as the case may be, they misapprehend the conditions, and set themselves to get it in some antinomian or legal way, and hence fail of any good result.

Others have the idea that obedience itself depends upon divine manifestations, and hence suppose they cannot obey till they get these manifestations. But this is not the Bible view of the subject. Our text says—If a man obey and love— then shall he have the manifestations—*then*, and not before.

Some set themselves to seek for these manifestations selfishly, for the luxury they may afford. Of course they fail of fulfilling the conditions and seek in vain. To seek these manifestations as some do that they may be distinguished and get honor to themselves, or if their motive be any other than the glory of God, the very seeking is an abomination to God, and will cause him to manifest to such seekers his wrath rather then his glory.

When persons set themselves to seek this blessing selfishly, they are commonly deluded by Satan, and suppose themselves to have obtained some great blessing when they have obtained no spiritual blessing at all. Satan, transformed in appearance to an angel of light deceives such men and makes them believe that God has revealed himself to them, when it is only the devil. This is my opinion as to such cases, and I will tell you why I think so. I have known several instances in which persons have related a most remarkable experience of most astonishing manifestations of God to the mind as they supposed; but the results were a bitter, hard, acrimonious spirit—a spirit of fierce denunciation instead of gentleness and love—a spirit such as the Holy Ghost never begets—but which is the genuine offspring of Satan's manifestations. Forthwith they plunge headlong into the most fantastical and absurd errors, and the most anti-christian practices. And yet in all these things, they will most pertinaciously insist that God is leading them. I have known several who gave up family prayer, and closet prayer, and yet insisted that God led them in all this. By the fruits we may know that it was not God but Satan who induced them to abandon prayer.

This is the history of their case. They learn from the Bible that God promises manifestations; from merely selfish motives they seek this blessing; and God answers them according to their seeking and his promise. They set up the idol of their own selfishness in their hearts, and seeking God thus, He answers them according to their idols as He has said he would. The Lord suffers Satan to deceive them. No wonder they are exceedingly positive and as bitter as they are positive. The hand of Satan is in all this. How else can you account for their state?

Yet let it be well considered—such cases do not at all impair the integrity of these promises, and ought not to shake our confidence in them. The false prophets revealed strange things; yet we know that this was the work of Satan. There were true prophets none the less, and their messages were none the less worthy of confidence. Real prophecies did not fail of coming to pass because Satan deceived some false prophets.

It is doubtful whether such persons are for any considerable time very positive that God is leading them, and that the manifestations they have are from him. Usually God gives them so much light that they *might*, if they would, see that their leader is not God but Satan. Sometimes under these Satanic hallucinations the mind is thrown from its balance. Such cases are an exception to the remark last made.

Again I remark, it is of vast importance that this doctrine respecting divine manifestations should be fully developed throughout all the church, and especially among all gospel ministers. Suppose that all ministers had these interviews with Christ and lived so near to him—nay rather, had Christ and the Father abiding continually in their hearts;—would they not preach as if they had a Savior and *knew* him? Would not all their preaching then be full of Christ, and would it not reveal Christ to their hearers? Verily they might then say with John, "That which we have seen and heard declare we unto you."

It is one of the greatest difficulties with ministers that they have lost this experience. They do not know Christ by the living experience of their hearts through his presence abiding within them. All that they can say about the gospel of Christ, they say upon mere faith as opposed to the clearer vision of these promised manifestations. All is mere faith and often very dim. O how much better to *see* Christ and be able to testify from the burning impressions made by such divine visions of Jesus!

It is indeed well to be able really and fully to believe that Christ is with us; but the mind needs greatly to *know* this and have it in the mind as a living, burning reality, kindling every energy of the soul by its presence and power. Every minister needs this in order to preach with energy and demonstration of the Spirit. The whole church needs it and must have it before she can be clothed again with the glory and power of apostolic days.

Many persons call these divine manifestations, sanctification. But this seems not to be the scriptural view. The Scriptures plainly represent obedience and love as the conditions, and these manifestations as consequent upon their being fulfilled. Of course sanctification precedes as a condition and is not merely an effect. At the same time it is doubtless true that these abiding revelations of Christ to the soul exert a most hallowing agency, and may well be called a spiritual cleansing. They do indeed rectify the sensibility, mightily quickening it towards God and his truth, and thus serve to purify the soul. To the individual Christian they are life from the dead, giving a glorious vitality to all his spiritual apprehensions. If they might only become general, they would be life from the dead to the whole world. If all the church were to come under this influence—if all missionaries went forth with this experience; if it were a universal fact among them that Christ manifested himself among them so that they should know him as they know each other, and be as conscious of his presence and of his guidance too as they ever are of a Christian brother's presence and counsel. O what tremendous power would this give to the whole missionary enterprize!

This gave the early apostles their great power. Driven by fierce persecution, they assemble together; Christ comes among them; the whole place is shaken where they are assembled together; they pray for a bold and fearless spirit that they may preach Christ in the face of scorn and scourging—and they have it. Nothing can daunt such men—and nothing stand before them.

It would be richly instructive to read this portion of the apostle's history with the eye on this point, and see what the results were of having such manifestations as they had on Christ, and such baptisms of the Holy Ghost.

This great blessing should be sought by every Christian. None should rest till he obtains it. Let his object in seeking it be the glory of God and his only; let him know that it is for the glory of God that he should have it, and that he cannot eminently glorify God without it—then let him know that if he will fulfill the conditions the blessing is surely given.

Every Christian is authorized to take this ground and ought to take it at once: If the conditions are within my power, as the Lord liveth, I will have it.

Let me say to those who doubt—this is the course you should pursue, for this will bring you the blessing you want. You need not be afraid to come to Christ and tell him all your difficulties; come in the simplicity and fulness of your heart and say, Lord thou knowest all things; thou knowest that I love thee; thou knowest it is in my heart to know and do all thy will; now come and manifest thyself unto me, and take up thine abode in my heart.

You need, brethren, only to seek these blessings with all your heart and you will obtain. I have been greatly struck with the fact that within the circle of my own observation these blessings are obtained of the Lord usually in this manner. Led by the Spirit of the Lord, an individual sets himself with great earnestness to mortify every lust and subdue every sin; he spares not his dearest idol; he loathes and abhors every thing that can separate his soul from his Savior, and puts it utterly away;—this being done his Savior comes and makes his gracious presence manifest. This is just what we might expect from Christ's language. When a Christian puts down every appetite and lust of body or mind that leads the heart away from Christ, and does all this for Christ, then let him know that he may lay hold of this promise of the Savior and say—Lord, I have humbly sought to fulfil all the conditions; now in thy mercy and faithfulness bestow on me the blessing." This is the remedy for doubting.

Then will the Savior come to your soul and reveal his glories. Then he will so attract your soul that you will cry after him in the spirit of adoption, entreating him to reveal himself yet more and more, until you can say—Surely the Lord hath done great things for me whereof I am glad and I will praise him; surely he hath done exceeding abundantly above all that I could ask or think; and to his name be all glory and praise forevermore.

Chapter VII.

ON PRAYER FOR THE HOLY SPIRIT.

Reported by Rev. Henry Cowles. May 23, 1855.

"If a son shall ask bread of any of you that is a father, will he give him a stone? or if he ask a fish, will he for a fish give him a serpent? Or, if he shall ask an egg, will he offer him a scorpion? If ye then, being evil, know how to give good gifts unto your children: how much more shall your heavenly Father give the Holy Spirit to them that ask him?"

Luke 11: 11-13.

These verses form the concluding part of a very remarkable discourse of our Lord to his disciples on prayer. It was introduced by their request that he would teach them how to pray. In answer to this request, he gave them what we are wont to call the Lord's Prayer, followed by a forcible illustration of the value of importunity, which he still further applied and enforced by renewing the general promise—"Ask and it shall be given you." Then, to confirm their faith still more, he expands the idea that God is their Father, and should be approached in prayer as if he were an infinitely kind and loving parent. This constitutes the leading idea in the strong appeal made in our text. "If a son shall ask bread of any of you that is a father, will he give him a stone? or, if he ask a fish, will he for a fish give him a serpent? Or, if he shall ask an egg, will he give him a scorpion? If ye then, being evil, know how to give good gifts unto your children, how much more shall your heavenly Father give the Holy Spirit to them that ask him?"

1. Remarking upon this text, I first observe that when we rightly understand the matter, we shall see that the gift of the Holy Ghost comprehends all we need spiritually. It secures to us that union with God which is eternal life. It implies

conversion, which consists in the will's being submitted to God's control. Sanctification is (1.) this union of the will to God perfected and perpetuated; (2.) the ascendancy of this state of the will over the entire sensibilities, so that the whole mind is drawn into union and sympathy with the mind and heart of God.

2. It is supremely easy to obtain this gift from God. In other words, it is easy to obtain from God all spiritual blessings that we truly need. If this be not so, what shall we think of these words of Christ? How can we by any means explain them consistently with fair truthfulness? Surely, it is easy for children to get really good things from their father. Which of you, being a father, does not know it to be easy for your children to get good things from you? You know in your own experience that they obtain without difficulty, even from you, all the real good they need, provided it be in your power to give it. But you are sometimes "evil," and Christ implies that, since God is never evil but always infinitely good, it is much more easy for one to get the Holy Spirit than even for your children to get bread from your hands. *"Much more!"* What words of meaning in such a connection as this! Every father knows there is nothing in the way of his children getting from him all the good things they really need and which he has to give. Every such parent values these good things for the sake of giving them to his children. For this, parents toil and plan for their children's sake. Can they then be averse or even slow to give these things to their children?

Yet God is much more ready to give his Spirit. My language, therefore, is not at all too strong. If God is much more ready and willing to give his children good things than you are to give to yours, then surely it must be easy and not difficult to get spiritual blessings, even to the utmost extent of our wants.

Let this argument come home to the hearts of those of you who are parents. Surely, you must feel its force. Christ must be a false teacher if this be not so. It must be that this great gift, which in itself comprehends all spiritual gifts, is most easily obtained, and in any amount which our souls need.

3. How very injurious and dishonorable to God are the practical views of almost all men on this subject! The dependence of men on the Holy Spirit has come to be the standing apology for moral and spiritual delinquency. Men every where profess to want the Holy Spirit, and more or less, to feel their need and to be praying for this gift; but continually and every where they complain that they do not get it. These complaints assume, both directly and indirectly, that it is very difficult to get this gift;—that God keeps his children on a very low diet; and on the smallest possible amount even of that; that he deals out their spiritual bread and water in most stinted amount—as if he purposed to keep his children only an inch above starvation. Pass among the churches and hear what they say and how they pray;—and what would you think? How would you be shocked at the strange, may I not say, *blasphemous* assumptions which they make concerning God's policy in giving, or rather *not* giving, the Holy Spirit to those that ask him! I can speak from experience and personal observation. When I began to attend prayer-meetings, this fact to which I have alluded struck me as very strange. I had never attended a prayer-meeting till I had come to manhood, for my situation in this respect was very unlike yours here. But after I came to manhood, and prayer-meetings were held in the place where I lived, I used to attend them very steadily. It was a matter of great interest to me, more than I can explain, or well express. I was filled with wonder to hear Christians pray, and the more so as I then began to read my Bible, and to find in it such things as we have in our text today. To read such promises, and then hear Christians talk was surprising. What they did say, coupled with what they seemed to mean, would run thus: I have a duty to perform at this meeting; I cannot go away without doing it. I

want to testify that religion is a good thing—a very good thing—although I have not got much of it. I believe God is a hearer of prayer, and yet I don't think he hears mine—certainly not to much purpose. I believe that prayer brings to us the Holy Spirit, and yet, though I have always been praying for this Spirit, I have scarcely ever received it.

Such seemed to be the strain of their talking and thinking, and I must say that it puzzled me greatly. I have reason to know that it has often puzzled others. Within a few years past, I have found this to be the standing objection of unconverted men. They say—"I cannot hold out if I should be converted—it is so difficult to get and to keep the Holy Spirit." They appeal to professed Christians and say, Look at them; they are not engaged in religion; they are not doing their Master's work in good earnest, and they confess it; they have not the Spirit, and they confess it; they bear a living testimony that these promises are of very little practical value.

Now, these are plain matters of fact, and should be deeply pondered by all professed Christians. The Christian life of multitudes is nothing less than a flat denial of the great truths of the Bible.

Often, when I am urging Christians to be filled with the Holy Ghost, I am asked—Do you really think this gift is for me? Do you think all can have it who will? If you tell them of instances, here and there, of persons who walk in the light, and are filled with the Spirit, they reply:—Are not those very special cases? Are they not the favored few, enjoying a blessing that only a few can hope to enjoy?

Here you should carefully observe, that the question is not whether few or many have this blessing; but—Is it practically within reach of all? Is it indeed available to all? Is the gift actually tendered to all in the fullest and highest sense? Is it easy to possess it? These being the real questions, we must see that the teachings of the text cannot be mistaken on this subject. Either Christ testified falsely of this matter, or this gift is available to all, and is easily obtained. For, of the meaning and scope of his language, there can be no doubt. No language can be plainer. No illustrations could be more clear, and none could easily be found that are stronger.

4. How shall we account for this impression, so extensively pervading the church, that the Holy Spirit can rarely be obtained in ample, satisfying fullness, and then only with the greatest difficulty?

This impression obviously grows out of the current experience of the church. In fact, but few seem to have this conscious communion with God through the Spirit; but few seem really to walk with God and be filled with his Spirit.

When I say *few*, I must explain myself to mean, few relatively to the whole number of professed Christians. Taken absolutely, the number is great and always has been. Sometimes, some have thought the number to be small, but they were mistaken. Elijah thought himself alone, but God gave him to understand that there were many—a host, spoken of as seven thousand—who had never bowed the knee to Baal. Ordinarily, such a use of the sacred number seven, is to be taken for a large, indefinite sum, much larger than if taken definitely. It may be so here. Even *then*, in that exceedingly dark age, there were yet many who stood unflinchingly for God.

It is a curious fact that persons who have really the most piety are often supposed to have the least, so few there are who judge of piety as God does. Those who preach the real gospel are often refreshed to find some in almost every congregation who manifestly embrace it. You can judge by their very looks,—their eyes shine and their faces are all aglow —almost like the face of Moses, descended from the mount.

But theirs is not the common experience of professed Christians. The common one which has served to create the general impression as to the difficulty of obtaining the Holy Spirit, is indeed utterly unlike this. The great body of nominal

Christians have not the Spirit, within the meaning of Romans 8th. They cannot say—"The law of the Spirit of life in Christ Jesus hath made me free from the law of sin and death." It is not true of them that they "walk not after the flesh, but after the Spirit." Comparatively few of all, know in their own conscious experience that they live and abide in the Spirit.

Here is another fact. Many are praying—apparently—for the Spirit of God, but do not get it. If you go to a prayer-meeting, you hear every body pray for this gift. It is so, also, in the family, and probably in the closet also. Yet, strange to tell, they do not get it. This experience of much prayer for this blessing, and much failure to get it, is every where common. Churches have their prayer-meetings, years and years in succession, praying for the Spirit, but they do not get it. In view of this fact, we must conclude, either that the promise is not reliable, or that the prayer does not meet the conditions of the promise. I shall take up this alternative by and by; just now, my business is to account for the prevalent impression that the Spirit of God is hard to get and keep, even in answer to prayer,—a fact which obviously is accounted for by the current experience of nominal Christians.

It should also be said that the churches have been taught that God is a sovereign, in such a sense that his gift of the Spirit is only occasional, and is then given without any connection with apparent causes—not dependent, by any means, on the fulfilment of conditions on our part. The common idea of sovereignty excludes the idea that God holds this blessing free to all, on condition of *real* prayer for it. I say real prayer, for I must show you by and by that much of the apparent praying of the church for the Spirit is not real prayer. It is this spurious selfish praying that leads to so much misconception as to the bestowment of the Holy Spirit.

Some of you may remember that I have related to you my experience at one time, when my mind was greatly exercised on this promise,—how I told the Lord I could not believe it. It was contrary to my conscious experience, and I could not believe any thing which contradicted my conscious experience. At that time the Lord kindly and in great mercy rebuked my unbelief, and showed me that the fault was altogether mine and in no part his.

Multitudes pray for the Spirit as I had done, and are in like manner disappointed because they do not get it. They are not conscious of being hypocrites; but they do not thoroughly know their own spirits. They think they are ready to make any sacrifices to obtain it. They do not seem to know that the difficulty is all with them. They fail to realize how rich and full the promise is. It all seems to them quite unaccountable that their prayer should not be answered. Often they sweat with agony of mind in their efforts to solve this mystery. They cannot bear to say that God's word is false, and they cannot see that it is true. It is apparently contradicted by their experience. This fact creates the agonizing perplexity.

5. In the next place, how can we reconcile this experience with Christ's veracity? How can we explain this experience according to the facts in the case, and yet show that Christ's teachings are to be taken in their obvious sense, and are strictly true?

I answer, what is here taught as to prayer must be taken in connection with what is taught elsewhere. For example, what is here said of asking must be taken in connection with what is said of praying in faith—with what is said by James of asking and not receiving because men ask amiss, that they may consume it upon their lusts. If any of you were to frame a will or a promissory note, binding yourself or your administrators to pay over certain moneys, on certain specified conditions, you would not think it necessary to state the conditions more than once. Having stated them distinctly once, you would go on to state in detail the promise; but you would not expect any body to separate the promise from the condition, and then claim the promise without having fulfilled the condition, and even perhaps accuse you of falsehood because you did not fulfil the promise when the conditions had not been met.

Now, the fact is that we find, scattered throughout the Bible, various revealed conditions of prayer. Whoever would pray acceptably must surely fulfil not merely a part, but all of these conditions. Yet in practice, the church, to a great extent, have overlooked, or at least has failed to meet these conditions. For example, they often pray for the Holy Spirit for selfish reasons. This is fearfully common. The real motives are selfish. Yet they come before God and urge their request often and long,—perhaps with great importunity; yet they are selfish in their very prayers, and God cannot hear. They are not in their inmost souls ready to do or to suffer all God's holy will. God calls some of his children through long seasons of extremest suffering, obviously as a means of purifying their hearts; yet many pray for pure hearts and for the Spirit to purify their hearts, who would rebel at once if God should answer their prayers by means of such a course of providence. Or, God may see it necessary to crucify your love of reputation, and for this end may subject you to a course of trial which will blow your reputation to the winds of heaven. Are you ready to hail the blessings of a subdued, unselfish heart, even though it be given by means of such discipline?

Often your motive in asking for the Spirit is merely personal comfort and consolation—as if you would live all your spiritual life on sweet-meats. Others ask for it really as a matter of self-glorification. They would like to have their names emblazoned in the papers. It would be so gratifying to be held up as a miracle of grace—as a most remarkable Christian. Alas, how many in various forms of it, are only offering selfish prayers! Even a minister might pray for the Holy Spirit from only sinister motives. He might wish to have it said that he is very spiritual, or a man of great spiritual power in his preaching or his praying; or he might wish to avoid that hard study to which a man who has not the Spirit must submit, since the Spirit does not teach him, nor give him unction. He might almost wish to be inspired, so easy would this gift make his preaching and his study. He might suppose that he really longed to be filled with the Spirit, while really he is only asking amiss, to consume it on some unhallowed desire. A student may pray for the Spirit to help him study, and yet only his ambition or his indolence may have inspired that prayer. Let it never be forgotten, we must sympathize with God's reasons for our having the Spirit, as we would hope to pray acceptably. There is nothing mysterious about this matter. The great end of all God's spiritual administrations towards us in providence or grace is to divest us of selfishness, and to bring our hearts into harmony with his in the spirit of real love.

Persons often quench the Spirit even while they are praying for it. One prays for the Spirit, yet that very moment, fails to notice the Spirit's monitions in his own breast, or refuses to do what the Spirit would lead and press him to do. Perhaps they even pray for the Spirit, that this gift may be a substitute for some self-denying duty to which the Spirit has long been urging them. This is no uncommon experience. Such persons will be very likely to think it very difficult to get the Spirit. A woman was going to a female prayer-meeting, and thought she wanted the Holy Spirit, and would make that her special errand at that meeting. Yet when there, the Spirit pressed her to pray audibly and she resisted, and excused herself.

It is common for persons to resist the Spirit in the very steps he chooses to take. They would make the Spirit yield to them; He would have them yield to him. They think only of having their blessings come in the way of their own choosing; He is wiser and will do it in his own way or not at all. If they cannot accept of his way, there can be no agreement. Often when persons pray for the Spirit, they have in their minds certain things which they would dictate to him as to the manner and circumstances. Such ought to know that if they would have the Spirit, they must accept Him in his own way.

Let him lead, and consider that your business is to follow. Thus it not infrequently happens that professed Christians maintain a perpetual resistance against the Holy Spirit, even while they are ostensibly praying for his presence and power. When He would fain draw them, they are thinking of dictating to him, and refuse to be led by him in his way. When they come really to understand what is implied in being filled with the Spirit, they draw back. It is more and different from what they had thought. *That* is not what they wanted.

REMARKS.

1. The difficulty is always and all of it, in us, not in God. You may write this down as a universal truth, from which there can be no exceptions.

2. The difficulty lies in our voluntary state of mind, and not in anything which is involuntary and beyond our control. Therefore, there is no excuse for our retaining it, and it should be at once given up.

There is no difficulty in our obtaining the Holy Spirit if we are willing to have it; but this implies a willingness to surrender ourselves to his direction and discretion.

3. We often mistake other states of mind for a willingness to have the Spirit of God. Nothing is more common than this. Men think they are willing to be filled with the Spirit, and to have that Spirit do all its own work in the soul; but they are really under a great mistake. To be willing to be wholly crucified to the world and the world unto us, is by no means common. Many think they have a sort of desire for this state, who would really shrink from it if they saw the reality near at hand. That persons do make continual mistakes and think themselves willing to be fully controlled by the Spirit, when they are not, is evident from their lives. The will governs the life, and therefore, the life must be an infallible index of the real state of the will. As is the life, so is the will, and therefore, when you see the life alien from God, you must

infer that the will is not wholly consecrated to his service—is not wholly in sympathy with God's will.

4. When the will is really on God's altar, entirely yielded up to God's will in all respects, one will not wait long ere he has the Spirit of God in the fullest measure. Indeed, this very consecration itself implies a large measure of the Spirit, yet not the *largest* measure. The mind may not be conscious of that deep union with God into which it may enter. The knowledge of God is a consciousness of God in the soul. You may certainly know that God's Spirit is within you, and that his light illumines your mind. His presence becomes a conscious reality.

The manner in which spiritual agencies, other than human manifest themselves in the mind of man, seems to some very mysterious. It is not necessary that we should know *how* those agencies get access to our minds; it suffices us to know beyond all question that they do. Christians sometimes know that the devil brings his own thoughts into the very chambers of their souls. Some of you have been painfully conscious of this. You have been certain that the devil has poured out his spirit upon you. Most horrid suggestions are thrust upon your mind—such as your inmost soul abhors, and such as could come from no other, and certainly from no *better*, source than the devil.

Now, if the devil can thus make us conscious of his presence and power, and can throw upon our souls his own horrid suggestions, may not the Spirit of God reveal his? Nay, if your heart is in sympathy with his suggestions and monitions, may He not do much more? Surely none can doubt that he can make his presence and agency a matter of positive consciousness. That must be a very imperfect and even false view of the case which supposes that we can be conscious of nothing but the operations of our own minds. Men are often conscious of Satan's thoughts, as present to their minds;—a fact which Bunyan well illustrated where he supposes Christian to be alarmed by some one whispering in his ear behind him, and pouring horrid blasphemies into his mind. Cases often occur like the following. A man came to me in great distress, saying, "I am no Christian; I know of a certainty. My mind has been filled with awful thoughts of God." But were those awful thoughts *your own* thoughts, and did you cherish them and give your assent to them? "No, indeed; nothing could have agonized me more." That is the work of the devil, said I. "Well," said he, "perhaps it is, and yet I had not thought of it so before."

So God's Spirit within us may become no less an object of our distinct consciousness. And if you do truly and earnestly wait on God, you shall be most abundantly supplied of his fullness.

5. To be filled with the Holy Ghost, so that he takes full possession of our souls, is what I mean by sanctification. This glorious work is wrought by the Spirit of God; and that Spirit never can take full and entire possession of our hearts without accomplishing this blessed work.

I do not wonder that those persons deny the existence of any such state as sanctification who do not know anything of being filled with the Holy Ghost. Ignoring his glorious agency, we need not wonder that they have no knowledge of his work in the soul.

6. Often the great difficulty in the way of Christian progress is an utter want of watchfulness. Some are so given to talking that they cannot hold communion with the Spirit of God. They have no leisure to listen to his "still small voice." Some are so fond of laughter, it seems impossible that their minds should ever be in a really serious frame. In such a mind, how can the Spirit of God dwell? Often in our Theological discussions, I am pained to see how difficult it is for persons engaged in dispute and mutual discussion, to avoid being chafed. Some of them are watchful and prayerful against this temptation, yet sometimes, we see persons manifestly fall

before this temptation. If Christians do not shut down the gate against all abuse of the tongue, and, indeed against every form of selfishness, there is no hope that they will resist the devil and the world so far as to be conquerors at last.

7. The Spirit of God troubles or comforts us, according as we resist or receive this great gift. The gospel scheme was purposed for the end of accomplishing this complete union and sympathy between our souls and God, so that the soul should enjoy God's own peace, and should be in the utmost harmony with its Maker and Father. Hence, it is the great business of the Spirit to bring about this state. If we concur, and if our will harmonizes with his efforts, he comforts us; if we resist, he troubles us;—a struggle ensues:—if, in this struggle, we come to understand God, and submit, then his blessings come freely and our peace is as a river; but so long as we resist, there can be no fruit of the Spirit's labor to us, but rebuke and trouble. To us he cannot be the author of peace and comfort.

8. How abominable to God it must be for the church to take ground, in regard to the Spirit, which practically denies the truth of this great promise in our text! How dreadful that Christians should hold and teach that it is a hard thing to be really religious! What abominable unbelief! How forcibly does the church thus testify *against* God before the world! You might as well burn your Bible as deny that it is the easiest thing in the world to get the gift of the Spirit. And yet, strange to tell, some hold that God is *so* sovereign, and is sovereign in such a sense, that few can get the Spirit at all, and those few only as it may happen, and not by any means as the result of provision freely made and promise reliably revealed on which any man's faith may take hold. O, how does this notion of sovereignty contradict the Bible! How long shall it be so?

Do you, young people, really believe that your young hearts may be filled with the Spirit? Do you really believe, as our text says, that God is more willing to give his Spirit to those that ask him, than your own father or mother would be to give you good things? Many of you are here, far from your parents. But you know that even your widowed mother, much as she may need every cent of her means for herself, would gladly share the last one with you if you needed it. So would your earthly father. Do you really believe that God is *as* willing as they—as ready—as loving? Nay, is he not *much more* so? as much more as he is better than your father or your mother? And now, do you really need and desire this gift of the Spirit? And if you do, will you come and ask for it in full confidence that you have a real *Father* in heaven?

Do you find practical difficulties? Do you realize how much you dishonor God if you refuse to believe his word of promise? Some of you say—I am so poor and so much in debt, I must go away and work somewhere and get money. But you have a father who has money enough. Yes; but he will not help me. He loves his money more than he loves his son. Would not this be a great scandal to your father—a living disgrace to him? Surely, it would;—and you would be so keenly sensible of this that you would not say it if it were not *very* true, nor then unless some very strong circumstances seemed to require of you the painful testimony. If your mother, being amply able, yet would not help you in your education or in your sickness, you would hardly tell of it—so greatly would it discredit her character.

And now will you have the face to say—God does not love me; he does not want to educate me for heaven; he utterly refuses to give me the Holy Spirit, although I often ask him and beseech him to do so? Will you even *think* this? And can you go even farther and act it out before all the world? O, why should you thus dishonor your own God and Father!

APPENDIX.

RELATIONS OF CHRIST TO THE BELIEVER.

Taken from Finney's Systematic Theology of 1851.
Covering chapters LXII to LXVI, pages 746 to 801
in the third volume of this series of
The Works of Charles G. Finney

For a fuller presentation of Finney's teaching on
entire sanctification, the baptism of the Holy Spirit,
or the higher life, see also chapters LVI to LXI
previous to those quoted below.

LECTURES LXII-LXVI.

SANCTIFICATION.

Conditions of entire sanctification.

To ascertain the conditions of entire sanctification in this life, we must consider what the temptations are that overcome us. When first converted, we have seen, that the heart or will consecrates itself and the whole being to God. We have also seen, that this is a state of disinterested benevolence, or a committal of the whole being to the promotion of the highest good of being. We have also seen, that all sin is selfishness, or that all sin consists in the will's seeking the indulgence or gratification of self; that it consists in the will's yielding obedience to the propensities, instead of obeying God, as his law is revealed in the reason. Now, who cannot see what needs to be done to break the power of temptation, and let the soul go free? The fact is, that the department of our sensibility that is related to objects of time and sense, has received an enormous development, and is tremblingly alive to all its correlated objects, while, by reason of the blindness of the mind to spiritual objects, it is scarcely developed at all in its relations to them. Those objects are seldom thought of by the carnal mind, and when they are, they are only thought of. They are not clearly seen, and of course they are not felt.

The thought of God, of Christ, of sin, of holiness, of heaven, and hell, excites little or no emotion in the carnal mind. The carnal mind is alive and awake to earthly and sensible objects, but dead to spiritual realities. The spiritual world needs to be revealed to the soul. The soul needs to see and clearly apprehend its own spiritual condition, relations, wants. It needs to become acquainted with God and Christ, to have spiritual and eternal realities made plain, and present, and all-absorbing realities to the soul. It needs such discoveries of the eternal world, of the nature and guilt of sin, and of Christ, the remedy of the soul, as to kill or greatly mortify lust, or the appetites and passions in their relations to objects of time and sense, and thoroughly to develope the sensibility, in its relations to sin and to God, and to the whole circle of spiritual realities. This will greatly abate the frequency and power of temptation to self-gratification, and break up the voluntary slavery of the will. The developements of the sensibility need to be thoroughly corrected. This can only be done by the revelation to the inward man, by the Holy Spirit, of those great, and solemn, and overpowering realities of the "spirit land," that lie concealed from the eye of flesh.

We often see those around us whose sensibility is so developed, in some one direction, that they are led captive by appetite and passion in that direction, in spite of reason and of God. The inebriate is an example of this. The glutton, the licentious, the avaricious man, &c., are examples of this kind. We sometimes, on the other hand, see, by some striking providence, such a counter developement of the sensibility produced, as to slay and put down those particular tendencies, and the whole direction of the man's life seems to be changed; and outwardly, at least, it is so. From being a perfect slave to his appetite for strong drink, he cannot, without the utmost loathing and disgust, so much as hear the name of his once loved beverage mentioned. From being a most avaricious man he becomes deeply disgusted with wealth, and spurns and despises it. Now, this has been effected by a counter developement of the sensibility; for, in the case supposed, religion has nothing to do with it. Religion does not consist in the states of the sensibility, nor in the will's being influenced by the sensibility; but sin consists in the will's being thus influenced. One great thing that needs to be done, to confirm and settle the will in the attitude of entire consecration to God, is to bring about a counter developement of the sensibility, so that it will not draw the will away from God. It needs to be mortified or crucified to the world, to objects of time and sense, by so deep, and clear, and powerful a revelation of self to self, and of Christ to the soul, as to awaken and develope all its susceptibilities in their relations to him, and to spiritual and divine realities. This can easily be done through and by the Holy Spirit, who takes of the things of Christ and shows them to us. He so reveals Christ, that the soul receives him to the throne of the heart, and to reign throughout the whole being. When the will, the intellect, and the sensibility are yielded to him, he develops the intelligence and the sensibility by clear revelations of himself, in all his offices and relations to the soul, confirms the will, mellows and chastens the sensibility, by these divine revelations to the intelligence.

It is plain, that men are naturally able to be entirely sanctified, in the sense of rendering entire and continual obedience to God; for the ability is the condition of the obligation to do so. But what is implied in ability to be as holy as God requires us to be?

The ready and plain answer to this question is—

1. The possession of the powers and susceptibilities of moral agents.

2. Sufficient knowledge or light to reveal to us the whole of duty.

3. And also to reveal to us clearly the way and means of overcoming any and every difficulty or temptation that lies in our way.

The first we all possess. The second we also possess, for nothing strictly is or can be duty, that is not revealed or made known to us. The third is proffered to us upon condition that we receive the Holy Spirit, who offers himself as an indwelling light and guide, and who is received by simple faith.

The light and grace which we need, and which it is the office of the Holy Spirit to supply, respects mainly the following things:—

(1.) Knowledge of ourselves, our past sins, their nature, aggravation, guilt, and desert of dire damnation.

(2.) Knowledge of our spiritual helplessness or weakness, in consequence of—

(i.) The physical depravity or morbid developement of our natures.

(ii.) Of the strength of selfish habit.

(iii.) Because of the power of temptation from the world, the flesh, and Satan.

(3.) We need the light of the Holy Spirit to teach us the character of God, the nature of his government, the purity of his law, the necessity and fact of atonement.

(4.) To teach us our need of Christ in all his offices and relations, governmental, spiritual, and mixed.

(5.) We need the revelation of Christ to our souls in all these relations, and in such power as to induce in us that appropriating faith, without which Christ is not, and cannot be, our salvation.

(6.) We need to know Christ, for example, in such relations as the following:—

(i.) As King, to set up his government and write his law in our hearts; to establish his kingdom within us; to sway his sceptre over our whole being. As King he must be spiritually revealed and received.

(ii.) As our Mediator, to stand between the offended justice of God and our guilty souls, to bring about a reconciliation between our souls and God. As Mediator he must be known and received.

(iii.) As our Advocate or *Paracletos*, our next or best friend, to plead our cause with the Father, our righteous and all-prevailing advocate to secure the triumph of our cause at the bar of God. In this relation he must be apprehended and embraced.

(iv.) As our Redeemer, to redeem us from the curse of the law, and from the power and dominion of sin; to pay the price demanded by public justice for our release, and to overcome and break up for ever our spiritual bondage. In this relation also we must know and appreciate him by faith.

(v.) As our Justification, to procure our pardon and acceptance with God. To know him and embrace him in this relation is indispensable to peace of mind and to release from the condemnation of the law.

(vi.) As our Judge, to pronounce sentence of acceptance, and to award to us the victor's crown.

(vii.) As the Repairer of the breach, or as the one who makes good to the government of God our default, or in other words, who, by his obedience unto death, rendered to the public justice of God a full governmental equivalent for the infliction of the penalty of the law upon us.

(viii.) As the Propitiation for our sins, to offer himself as a propitiatory or offering for our sins. The apprehension of Christ as making an atonement for our sins seems to be indispensable to the entertaining of a healthy hope of eternal life. It certainly is not healthy for the soul to apprehend the mercy of God, without regarding the conditions of its exercise. It does not sufficiently impress the soul with a sense of the justice and holiness of God, with the guilt and desert of sin. It does not sufficiently awe the soul and humble it in the deepest dust, to regard God as extending pardon, without regard to the sternness of his justice, as evinced in requiring that sin should be recognized in the universe, as worthy of the wrath and curse of God, as a condition of its forgiveness. It is remarkable, and well worthy of all consideration, that those who deny the atonement make sin a comparative trifle, and seem to regard God's benevolence or love as good nature, rather than, as it is, "a consuming fire" to all the workers of iniquity. Nothing does or can produce that awe of God, that fear and holy dread of sin, that self-abasing, God-justifying spirit, that a thorough apprehension of the atonement of Christ will do. Nothing like this can beget that spirit of self-renunciation, of cleaving to Christ, of taking refuge in his blood. In these relations Christ must be revealed to us, and apprehended and embraced by us, as the condition of our entire sanctification.

(ix.) As the Surety of a better than the first covenant, that is, as surety of a gracious covenant founded on better promises; as an underwriter or endorser of our obligation: as one who undertakes for us, and pledges himself as our security, to fulfil for and in us all the conditions of our salvation. To apprehend and appropriate Christ by faith in this relation, is no doubt, a condition of our entire sanctification. I should greatly delight to enlarge, and write a whole course of lectures on the offices and relations of Christ, the necessity of knowing and appropriating him in these relations, as the condition of our entire, in the sense of continued sanctification. This would require a large volume. All that I can do is merely to suggest a skeleton outline of this subject in this place.

(x.) We need to apprehend and appropriate Christ as dying for our sins. It is the work of the Holy Spirit thus to reveal his death in its relations to our individual sins, and as related to our sins as individuals. The soul needs to apprehend Christ as crucified for us. It is one thing for the soul to regard the death of Christ merely as the death of a martyr, and an infinitely different thing, as every one knows, who has had the experience, to apprehend his death as a real and veritable vicarious sacrifice for our sins, as being truly a substitute for our death. The soul needs to apprehend Christ as suffering on the cross for it, or as its substitute; so that it can say, That sacrifice is for me, that suffering and that death are for my sins; that blessed Lamb is slain for my sins. If thus fully to apprehend and to appropriate Christ cannot kill sin in us, what can?

(xi.) We also need to know Christ as risen for our justification. He arose and lives to procure our certain acquittal, or our complete pardon and acceptance with God. That he lives, and is our justification we need to know, to break the bondage of legal motives, and to slay all selfish fear; to break and destroy the power of temptation from this source. The clearly convinced soul is often tempted to despondency and unbelief, to despair of its own acceptance with God, and it would surely fall into the bondage of fear, were it not for the faith of Christ as a risen, living, justifying Saviour. In this relation, the soul needs clearly to apprehend and fully to appropriate Christ in his completeness, as a condition of abiding in a state of disinterested consecration to God.

(xii.) We need also to have Christ revealed to us as bearing our griefs and as carrying our sorrows. The clear apprehension of Christ, as being made sorrowful for us, and as bending under sorrows and griefs which in justice belonged to us, tends at once to render sin unspeakably odious, and Christ infinitely precious to our souls. The idea of Christ our substitute, needs to be thoroughly developed in our minds. And this relation of Christ needs to be so clearly revealed to us, as to become an everywhere present reality to us. We need to have Christ so revealed as to so completely ravish and engross our affections, that we would sooner die at once than sin against him. Is such a thing impossible? Indeed it is not. Is not the Holy Spirit able, and willing, and ready thus to reveal him, upon condition of our asking it in faith? Surely he is.

(xiii.) We also need to apprehend Christ as the one by whose stripes we are healed. We need to know him as relieving our pains and sufferings by his own, as preventing our death by his own, as sorrowing that we might eternally rejoice, as grieving that we might be unspeakably and eternally glad, as dying in unspeakable agony that we might die in deep peace and in unspeakable triumph.

(xiv.) "As being made sin for us." We need to apprehend him as being treated as a sinner, and even as the chief of sinners on our account, or for us. This is the representation of scripture, that Christ on our account was treated as if he were a sinner. He was made sin for us, that is, he was treated as a sinner, or rather as being the representative, or as it were the embodiment of sin for us. O! this the soul needs to apprehend—the holy Jesus treated as a sinner, and as if all sin were concentrated in him, on our account! We procured this treatment of him. He consented to take our place in such a sense as to endure the cross, and the curse of the law for us. When the soul apprehends this, it is ready to die with grief and love. O how infinitely it loathes self under such an apprehension as this! In this relation he must not only be apprehended, but appropriated by faith.

(xv.) We also need to apprehend the fact that "he was made sin for us, that we might be made the righteousness of God in him;" that Christ was treated as a sinner, that we might be treated as righteous; that we might also be made personally righteous by faith in him; that we might be made the "righteousness of God in him;" that we might inherit and be made partakers of God's righteousness, as that righteousness exists and is revealed in Christ; that we might in and by him be made righteous as God is righteous. The soul needs to see, that his being made sin for us, was in order that we might be "made the righteousness of God in him." It needs to embrace and lay hold by faith upon that righteousness of God, which is brought home to saints in Christ, through the atonement and indwelling Spirit.

(xvi.) We also need him revealed to the soul, as one upon whose shoulders is the government of the world; who administers the government, moral and providential, of this world, for the protection, discipline, and benefit of believers. This revelation has a most sin-subduing tendency. That all events are directly or indirectly controlled by him who has so loved us as to die for us; that all things absolutely are designed for, and will surely result in our good. These and such like considerations, when revealed to the soul and made living realities by the Holy Spirit, tend to kill selfishness and confirm the love of God in the soul.

(xvii.) We also need Christ revealed to the inward being, as "head over all things to the church." All these relations are of no avail to our sanctification, only in so far forth as they are directly, and inwardly, and personally revealed to the soul by the Holy Spirit. It is one thing to have thoughts, and ideas, and opinions concerning Christ, and an entirely different thing to know Christ, as he is revealed by the Holy Spirit. All the relations of Christ imply corresponding necessities in us. When the Holy Spirit has revealed to us the necessity, and Christ as exactly suited to fully meet that necessity, and urged his acceptance in that relation, until we have appropriated him by faith, a great work is done. But until we are thus revealed to ourselves, and Christ is thus revealed to us and accepted by us, nothing is done more than to store our heads with notions or opinions and theories, while our hearts are becoming more and more, at every moment, like an adamant stone.

I have often feared, that many professed Christians knew Christ only after the flesh, that is, they have no other knowledge of Christ than what they obtain by reading and hearing about him, without any special revelation of him to the inward being by the Holy Spirit. I do not wonder, that such professors and ministers should be totally in the dark, upon the subject of entire sanctification in this life. They regard sanctification as brought about by the formation of holy habits, instead of resulting from the revelation of Christ to the soul in all his fulness and relations, and the soul's renunciation of self and appropriation of Christ in these relations. Christ is represented in the Bible as the head of the church. The church is represented as his body. He is to the church what the head is to the body. The head is the seat of the intellect, the will, and in short, of the living soul. Consider what the body would be without the head, and you may understand what the church would be without Christ. But as the church would be without Christ, so each believer would be without Christ. But we need to have our necessities in this respect clearly revealed to us by the Holy Spirit, and this relation of Christ made plain to our apprehension. The utter darkness of the human mind in regard to its own spiritual state and wants, and in regard to the relations and fulness of Christ, is truly wonderful. His relations, as mentioned in the Bible, are overlooked almost entirely until our wants are discovered. When these are made known, and the soul begins in earnest to inquire after a remedy, it needs not inquire in vain. "Say not in thine heart, who shall ascend up to heaven? that is, to bring Christ down from above; or who shall descend into the deep? that is, to bring Christ again from the dead. But what saith it? The word is nigh thee, even in thy mouth, and in thy heart."

(xviii.) Christ, as having all power or authority in heaven and earth, needs also to be revealed to the soul, and received by faith, to dwell in and rule over it. The corresponding want must of necessity be first known to the mind, before it can apprehend and appropriate Christ by faith, in this or any other relation. The soul needs to see and feel its weakness, its need of protection, of being defended, and watched over, and controlled. It needs to see this, and also the power of its spiritual enemies, its besetments, its dangers, and its certain ruin, unless the Almighty One interpose in its behalf. It needs thus truly and deeply to know itself; and then, to inspire it with confidence, it needs a revelation of Christ as God, as the Almighty God, to the soul, as one who possesses absolute and infinite power, and as presented to the soul to be accepted as its strength, and as all it needs of power.

O how infinitely blind he is to the fulness and glory of Christ, who does not know himself and Christ as both are revealed by the Holy Spirit. When we are led by the Holy

Spirit to look down into the abyss of our own emptiness—to behold the horrible pit and miry clay of our own habits, and fleshly, and worldly, and infernal entanglements; when we see in the light of God, that our emptiness and necessities are infinite; then, and not till then, are we prepared wholly to cast off self, and to put on Christ. The glory and fulness of Christ are not discovered to the soul, until it discovers its need of him. But when self, in all its loathsomeness and helplessness, is fully revealed, until hope is utterly extinct, as it respects every kind and degree of help in ourselves; and when Christ, the all and in all, is revealed to the soul as its all-sufficient portion and salvation, then, and not until then, does the soul know its salvation. This knowledge is the indispensable condition of appropriating faith, or of that act of receiving Christ, or that committal of all to him, that takes Christ home to dwell in the heart by faith, and to preside over all its states and actions. O, such a knowledge and such a reception and putting on of Christ is blessed. Happy is he who knows it by his own experience.

It is indispensable to a steady and implicit faith, that the soul should have a spiritual apprehension of what is implied in the saying of Christ, that all power was delivered unto him. The ability of Christ to do all, and even exceeding abundantly above all that we ask or think, is what the soul needs clearly to apprehend in a spiritual sense, that is, to apprehend it, not merely as a theory or as a proposition, but to see the true spiritual import of this saying. This is also equally true of all that is said in the Bible about Christ, of all his offices and relations. It is one thing to theorize, and speculate, and opine, about Christ, and an infinitely different thing to know him as he is revealed by the Holy Spirit. When Christ is fully revealed to the soul by the Comforter, it will never again doubt the attainability and reality of entire sanctification in this life.

(xix.) Another necessity of the soul is to know Christ spiritually, as the Prince of Peace. "Peace I leave with you; my peace I give unto you," said Christ. What is this peace? And who is Christ, in the relation of the Prince of Peace? What is it to possess the peace of Christ—to have the peace of God rule in our hearts? Without the revelation of Christ to the soul by the Holy Spirit, it has no spiritual apprehension of the meaning of this language. Nor can it lay hold on and appropriate Christ as its peace, as the Prince of Peace. Whoever knows and has embraced Christ as his peace, and as the Prince of Peace, knows what it is to have the peace of God rule in his heart. But none else at all understand the true spiritual import of this language, nor can it be so explained to them as that they will apprehend it, unless it be explained by the Holy Spirit.

(xx.) The soul needs also to know Christ as the Captain of salvation, as the skilful conductor, guide, and captain of the soul in all its conflicts with its spiritual enemies, as one who is ever at hand to lead the soul on to victory, and make it more than a conqueror in all its conflicts with the world, the flesh, and Satan. How indispensable to a living and efficient faith it is and must be, for the soul clearly to apprehend by the Holy Spirit this relation of Captain of Salvation, and Captain of the Lord's Host. Without confidence in the Leader and Captain, how shall the soul put itself under his guidance and protection in the hour of conflict? It cannot.

The fact is, that when the soul is ignorant of Christ as a Captain or Leader, it will surely fall in battle. If the church, as a body, but knew Christ as the Captain of the Lord's Host; if he were but truly and spiritually known to them in that relation, no more confusion would be seen in the ranks of God's elect. All would be order, and strength, and conquest. They would soon go up and take possession of the whole territory that has been promised to Christ. The heathen would soon be given to him for an inheritance, and the uttermost parts of the world for a possession. Joshua knew Christ as the Captain of the Lord's host. Consequently he had more courage, and efficiency, and prowess, than all Israel besides. Even so it is now. When a soul can be found who thoroughly knows, and has embraced, and appropriated Christ, he is a host of himself. That is, he has appropriated the attributes of Christ to himself; and his influence is felt in heaven, and earth, and hell.

(xxi.) Another affecting and important relation in which the soul needs to know Christ, is that of our Passover. It needs to understand, that the only reason why it has not been, or will not assuredly be, slain for sin is, that Christ has sprinkled, as our Paschal Lamb, the lintel and door-posts of our souls with his own blood, and that therefore the destroying angel passes us by. There is a most deep and sin-subduing, or rather temptation-subduing spirituality in this relation of Christ to the soul, when revealed by the Holy Spirit. We must apprehend our sins as slaying the Lamb, and apply his blood to our souls by faith—his blood as being our protection and our only trust. We need to know the security there is in this being sprinkled with his blood, and the certain and speedy destruction of all who have not taken refuge under it. We need to know also, that it will not do for a moment to venture out into the streets, and from under its protection, lest we be slain there.

(xxii.) To know Christ as our Wisdom, in the true spiritual sense, is doubtless indispensable to our entire, in the sense of continued, sanctification. He is our wisdom, in the sense of being the whole of our religion. That is, when separated from him, we have no spiritual life whatever. He is at the bottom of, or the inducing cause of all our obedience. This we need clearly to apprehend. Until the soul clearly understands this, it has learned nothing to the purpose of its helplessness, and of Christ's spiritual relations to it.

(xxiii.) Very nearly allied to this is Christ's relation to the soul as its Sanctification. I have been amazed at the ignorance of the church and of the ministry, respecting Christ as its Sanctification. He is not its Sanctifier in the sense that he does something to the soul that enables it to stand and persevere in holiness in its own strength. He does not change the structure of the soul, but he watches over, and works in it to will and to do continually, and thus becomes its Sanctification. His influence is not exerted once for all, but constantly. When he is apprehended and embraced as the soul's Sanctification, he rules in, and reigns over the soul in so high a sense, that he, as it were, developes his own holiness in us. He, as it were, swallows us up, so enfolds, if I may so say, our wills and our souls in his, that we are willingly led captive by him. We will and do as he wills within us. He charms the will into a universal bending to his will. He so establishes his throne in, and his authority over us, that he subdues us to himself. He becomes our sanctification only in so far forth as we are revealed to ourselves, and he revealed to us, and as we receive him and put him on. What! has it come to this, that the church doubts and rejects the doctrine of entire sanctification in this life? Then, it must be that it has lost sight of Christ as its sanctification. Is not Christ perfect in all his relations? Is there not a completeness and fulness in him? When embraced by us, are we not complete in him? The secret of all this doubting about, and opposition to, the doctrine of entire sanctification, is to be found in the fact, that Christ is not apprehended and embraced as our sanctification. The Holy Spirit sanctifies only by revealing Christ to us as our sanctification. He does not speak of himself, but takes of the things of Christ and shows them to us. Two among the most prominent ministers in the presbyterian church have said to me within a few years, that they had never heard of Christ as the sanctification of the soul. O, how many of the ministry of the present day overlook the true spiritual gospel of Christ!

(xxiv.) Another of Christ's spiritual relations is that of the Redemption of the soul; not merely as the Redeemer considered in his governmental relation, but as a present Redemption. To apprehend and receive Christ in this relation, the soul needs to apprehend itself as sold under sin; as being the voluntary but real slave of lust and appetite, except as Christ continually delivers us from its power, by strengthening and confirming our wills in resisting and overcoming the flesh.

(xxv.) Christ our Prophet is another important spiritual relation in which we need to apprehend Christ by the Holy Spirit, as a condition of entire sanctification. He must be received as the great teacher of our souls, so that every word of his will be received as God speaking to us. This will render the Bible precious, and all the words of life efficient to the sanctification of our souls.

(xxvi.) As our High Priest, we need also to know Christ. I say we need to know him in this relation, as really ever living and ever sustaining this relation to us, offering up, as it were, by a continual offering, his own blood, and himself as a propitiation for our sins; as being entered within the veil, and as ever living to make intercession for us. Much precious instruction is to be gathered from this relation of Christ. We need, perishingly need, to know Christ in this relation, as a condition of a right dependence upon him. I all the while feel embarrassed with the consideration that I am not able, in this course of instruction, to give a fuller account of Christ in these relations. We need a distinct revelation of him in each of these relations, in order to a thorough understanding and clear apprehension of that which is implied in each and all of the relations of Christ.

When we sin, it is because of our ignorance of Christ. That is, whenever temptation overcomes us, it is because we do not know and avail ourselves of the relation of Christ that would meet our necessities. One great thing that needs to be done is, to correct the developements of our sensibility. The appetites and passions are enormously developed in their relations to earthly objects. In relation to things of time and sense, our propensities are greatly developed and are alive; but in relation to spiritual truths and objects, and eternal realities, we are naturally as dead as stones. When first converted, if we knew enough of ourselves and of Christ thoroughly to develope and correct the action of the sensibility, and confirm our wills in a state of entire consecration, we should not fall. In proportion as the law-work preceding conversion has been thorough, and the revelation of Christ at, or immediately subsequent to, conversion, full and clear, just in that proportion do we witness stability in converts. In most, if not in all instances, however, the convert is too ignorant of himself, and of course knows too little about Christ, to be established in permanent obedience. He needs renewed conviction of sin, to be revealed to himself, and to have Christ revealed to him, and be formed in him the hope of glory, before he will be steadfast, always abounding in the work of the Lord.

Before I close this lecture, I must remark, and shall have occasion to repeat the remark, that from what has been said, it must not be inferred, that the knowledge of Christ in all these relations is a condition of our coming into a state of entire consecration to God, or of present sanctification. The thing insisted on is, that the soul will abide in this state in the hour of temptation only so far forth as it betakes itself to Christ in such circumstances of trial, and apprehends and appropriates him by faith from time to time in those relations that meet the present and pressing necessities of the soul. The temptation is the occasion of revealing the necessity, and the Holy Spirit is always ready to reveal Christ in the particular relation suited to the newly-developed necessity. The perception and appropriation of him in this relation, under these circumstances of trial, is the *sine quà non* of our remaining in the state of entire consecration.

(xxvii.) We need also to know ourselves as starving souls, and Christ as the "bread of life," as "the bread that came down from heaven." We need to know spiritually and experimentally what it is to "eat of his flesh, and to drink of his blood," to receive him as the bread of life, to appropriate him to the nourishment of our souls as really as we appropriate bread, by digestion, to the nourishment of our bodies. This I know is mysticism to the carnal professor. But to the truly spiritually-minded, "this is the bread of God that came down from heaven, of which if a man eat he shall never die." To hear Christ talk of eating his flesh, and of drinking his blood, was a great stumbling-block to the carnal Jews, as it now is to carnal professors. Nevertheless, this is a glorious truth, that Christ is the constant sustenance of the spiritual life, as truly and as literally as food is the sustenance of the body. But the soul will never eat this bread until it has ceased to attempt to fill itself with the husks of its own doings, or with any provision this world can furnish. Do you know, Christian, what it is to eat of this bread? If so, then you shall never die.

(xxviii.) Christ also needs to be revealed to the soul as the fountain of the water of life. "If any man thirst," says he, "let him come unto me and drink." "I am Alpha and Omega, the beginning and the end. To him that is athirst, I will give unto him of the fountain of the water of life freely." The soul needs to have such discoveries made to it, as to beget a thirst after God that cannot be allayed, except by a copious draught at the fountain of the water of life. It is indispensable to the establishing of the soul in perfect love, that its hungering after the bread, and its thirsting for the water of life, should be duly excited, and that the spirit should pant and struggle after God, and "cry out for the living God," that it should be able to say with truth: "My soul panteth for God as the hart panteth for the water-brooks; My heart and my flesh crieth out for the living God;" "My soul breaketh for the longing that it hath after thee at all times." When this state of mind is induced by the Holy Spirit, so that the longing of the soul after perpetual holiness is irrepressible, it is prepared for a revelation of Christ, in all those offices and relations that are necessary to secure its establishment in love. Especially is it then prepared to apprehend, appreciate, and appropriate Christ, as the bread and water of life, to understand what it is to eat the flesh and drink the blood of the Son of God. It is then in a state to understand what Christ meant when he said, "Blessed are they that do hunger and thirst after righteousness, for they shall be filled." They not only understand what it is to hunger and thirst, but also what it is to be filled; to have the hunger and thirst allayed, and the largest desire fully satisfied. The soul then realizes in its own experience the truthfulness of the apostle's saying, that Christ "is able to do exceeding abundantly above all that we ask or think." Many stop short even of anything like intense hunger and thirst; others hunger and thirst, but have not the idea of the perfect fulness and adaptedness of Christ to meet and satisfy the longing of their souls. They therefore do not plead and look for the soul-satisfying revelation of Christ. They expect no such divine fulness and satisfaction of soul. They are ignorant of the fulness and perfection of the provisions of the "glorious gospel of the blessed God;" and consequently they are not encouraged to hope from the fact, that they hunger and thirst after righteousness, that they shall be filled; but they remain unfed, unfilled, unsatisfied, and after a season, through unbelief, fall into indifference, and remain in bondage to sin.

(xxix.) The soul needs also to know Christ as the true God, and the eternal life. "No man can say that Jesus is the Lord, save by the Holy Spirit." The proper divinity of Christ is never, and never can be, held otherwise than as a mere opinion, a tenet, a speculation, an article of creed, until he is revealed to the inner man by the Holy Spirit. But nothing short of an apprehension of Christ, as the supreme and living God to the soul, can inspire that confidence in him that is essential to its established sanctification. The soul can have no apprehension of what is intended by his being the "eternal life," until it spiritually knows him as the true God. When he is spiritually revealed as the true and living God, the way is prepared for the spiritual apprehension of him as the eternal life. "As the living Father hath life in himself, so hath he given to the Son to have life in himself." "In him was life, and the life was the light of men." "I give unto them eternal life." "I am the way, the truth, and the life." "I am the resurrection and the life." These and similar passages the soul needs spiritually to apprehend, to have a spiritual and personal revelation of them within. Most professors seem to me to have no right idea of the condition upon which the Bible can be made of spiritual use to them. They seem not to understand, that in its letter it is only a history of things formerly revealed to men; that it is, in fact, a revelation to no man, except upon the condition of its being personally revealed, or revealed to us in particular by the Holy Spirit. The mere fact, that we have in the gospel the history of the birth, the life, the death of Christ, is no such revelation of Christ to any man as meets his necessities; and as will secure his salvation. Christ and his doctrine, his life, and death, and resurrection, need to be revealed personally by the Holy Spirit, to each and every soul of man, to effect his salvation. So it is with every spiritual truth; without an inward revelation of it to the soul, it is only a savour of death unto death. It is in vain to hold to the proper divinity of Christ, as a speculation, a doctrine, a theory, an opinion, without the revelation of his divine nature and character to the soul, by the Holy Spirit. But let the soul know him, and walk with him as the true God, and then it will no longer question whether, as our sanctification, he is all-sufficient and complete. Let no one object to this, that if this is true, men are under no obligation to believe in Christ, and to obey the gospel, without or until they are enlightened by the Holy Spirit. To such an objection, should it be made, I would answer,—

(*a.*) Men are under an obligation to believe every truth so far as they can understand or apprehend it, but no further. So far as they can apprehend the spiritual truths of the gospel without the Holy Spirit, so far, without his aid, they are bound to believe it. But Christ has himself taught us, that no man can come to him except the Father draw him. That this drawing means teaching is evident, from what Christ proceeds to say. "For it is written," said he, "they shall all be taught of God. Every one therefore that hath heard and hath learned of the Father cometh unto me." That this learning of the Father is something different from the mere oral or written instructions of Christ and the apostles, is evident from the fact, that Christ assured those to whom he preached, with all the plainness with which he was able, that they still could not come to him except drawn, that is taught, of the Father. As the Father teaches by the Holy Spirit, Christ's plain teaching, in the passage under consideration is, that no man can come to him except he be specially enlightened by the Holy Spirit. Paul unequivocally teaches the same thing. "No man," says he, "can say that Jesus is the Lord, but by the Holy Spirit." Notwithstanding all the teaching of the apostles, no man by merely listening to their instruction could so apprehend the true divinity of Christ, as honestly and with spiritual understanding to say, that Jesus is the Lord. But what spiritual or true Christian does not know the radical difference between being taught of man and of God, between the opinions that we form from reading, hearing, and study, and the clear apprehensions of truths that are communicated by the direct and inward illuminations of the Holy Spirit.

(*b.*) I answer, that men under the gospel are entirely without excuse for not enjoying all the light they need from the Holy Spirit, since he is in the world, has been sent for the very purpose of giving to men all the knowledge of themselves and of Christ which they need. His aid is freely proffered to all, and Christ has assured us, that the Father is more willing to give the Holy Spirit to them that ask him, than parents are to give good gifts to their children. All men under the gospel know this, and all men have light enough to ask in faith for the Holy Spirit, and of course all men may know of themselves and of Christ all that they need to know. They are therefore able to know and to embrace Christ as fully and as fast as it is their duty to embrace him. They are able to know Christ in his governmental and spiritual relations, just as fast as they come into circumstances to need to know him in these various relations. The Holy Spirit, if he is not quenched and resisted, will surely reveal Christ in all his relations in due time, so that, in every temptation a way of escape will be open, so that we shall be able to bear it. This is expressly promised, 1 Cor. x. 13, "There hath no temptation taken you but such as is common to man; but God is faithful, who will not suffer you to be tempted above that ye are able, but will with the temptation also make a way to escape, that ye may be able to bear it." Men are able to know what God offers to teach them, upon a condition within the compass of their ability. The Holy Spirit offers, upon condition of faith in the express promise of God, to lead every man into all truth. Every man is, therefore, under obligation to know and do the whole truth, so far and so fast as it is possible for him to do so, with the light of the Holy Spirit.

(xxx.) But be it remembered, that it is not enough for us to apprehend Christ as the true God and the eternal life, but we need also to lay hold upon him as our life. It cannot be too distinctly understood, that a particular and personal appropriation of Christ, in such relations, is indispensable to our being rooted and grounded, established and perfected in love. When our utter deficiency and emptiness in any one respect or direction, is deeply revealed to us by the Holy Spirit, with the corresponding remedy and perfect fulness in Christ, it then remains for the soul, in this respect and direction, to cast off self, and put on Christ. When this is done, when self in that respect and direction is dead, and Christ is risen, and lives and reigns in the heart in that relation, all is strong, and whole, and complete, in that department of our life and experience. For example, suppose we find ourselves constitutionally, or by reason of our relations and circumstances, exposed to certain besetments and temptations that overcome us. Our weakness in this respect we observe in our experience. But upon observing our exposedness, and experiencing something of our weakness, we begin with piling resolution upon resolution. We bind ourselves with oaths and promises, and covenants, but all in vain. When we purpose to stand, we invariably, in the presence of the temptation, fall. This process of resolving and falling brings the soul into great discouragement and perplexity, until at last the Holy Spirit reveals to us fully, that we are attempting to stand and to build upon nothing. The utter emptiness and worse than uselessness of our resolutions and self-originated efforts, is so clearly seen by us, as to annihilate for ever self-dependence in this respect. Now the soul is prepared for the revelation of Christ to meet this particular want. Christ is revealed and apprehended as the soul's substitute, surety, life, and salvation, in respect to the particular besetment and weakness of which it has had so full and so humiliating a revelation. Now, if the soul utterly and for ever casts off and renounces self, and puts on the Lord Jesus Christ, as he is seen to be needed to meet his necessity, then all is complete in him. Thus far Christ is reigning within us. Thus far we know what is the power of his resurrection, and are made conformable to his death.

But I said, that we need to know and to lay hold upon Christ as our life. Too much stress cannot be laid upon our personal responsibility to Christ, our individual relation to him, our personal interest in him, and obligation to him. To sanctify our own souls, we need to make every department of religion a personal matter between us and God, to regard every precept of the Bible, and every promise, saying, exhortation, threatening, and in short, we need to regard the whole Bible as given to us, and earnestly seek the personal revelation of every truth it contains to our own souls. No one can too fully understand, or too deeply feel, the necessity of taking home the Bible with all it contains, as a message sent from Heaven to him; nor can too earnestly desire or seek the promised Spirit to teach him the true spiritual import of all its contents. He must have the Bible made a personal revelation of God to his own soul. It must become his own book. He must know Christ for himself. He must know him in his different relations. He must know him in his blessed and infinite fulness, or he cannot abide in him, and unless he abide in Christ, he can bring forth none of the fruits of holiness. "Except a man abide in me, he is cast forth as a branch, and is withered."

Apprehending and embracing Christ as our life implies the apprehension of the fact, that we of ourselves are dead in trespasses and in sins, that we have no life in ourselves, that death has reigned, and will eternally reign in and over us, unless Christ become our life. Until man knows himself to be dead, and that he is wholly destitute of spiritual life in himself, he will never know Christ as his life. It is not enough to hold the opinion, that all men are by nature dead in trespasses and sins. It is not enough to hold the opinion, that we are, in common with all men, in this condition in and of ourselves. We must see it. We must know what such language means. It must be made a matter of personal revelation to us. We must be made fully to apprehend our own death, and Christ as our life; and we must fully recognize our death and him as our life, by personally renouncing self, in this respect, and laying hold on him as our own spiritual and eternal life. Many persons, and, strange to say, some eminent ministers, are so blinded as to suppose, that a soul entirely sanctified does not any longer need Christ, assuming that such a soul has spiritual life in and of himself; that there is in him some foundation or efficient occasion of continued holiness, as if the Holy Spirit had changed his nature, or infused physical holiness or an independent holy principle into him, in such a sense that they have an independent well-spring of holiness within, as a part of themselves. Oh, when will such men cease to darken counsel by words without knowledge, upon the infinitely important subject of sanctification! When will such men—when will the church, understand that Christ is our sanctification; that we have no life, no holiness, no sanctification, except as we abide in Christ, and he in us; that, separate from Christ, there never is any moral excellence in any man; that Christ does not change the constitution of man in sanctification, but that he only, by our own consent, gains and keeps the heart; that he enthrones himself, with our consent, in the heart, and through the heart extends his influence and his life to all our spiritual being; that he lives in us as really and truly as we live in our own bodies; that he as really reigns in our will, and consequently in our emotions, by our own free consent, as our wills reign in our bodies? Cannot our brethren understand, that this is sanctification, and that nothing else is? that there is no degree of sanctification that is not to be thus ascribed to Christ? and that entire sanctification is nothing else than the reign of Jesus in the soul? nothing more nor less than Christ, the resurrection and the life, raising the soul from spiritual death, and reigning in it through righteousness unto eternal life? I must know and embrace Christ as my life; I must abide in him as a branch abides in the vine; I must not only hold this as an opinion; I must know and act on it in practice. Oh, when the ministry of reconciliation all know and embrace a whole Christ for themselves; when they preach Jesus in all his fulness and present vital power to the church; when they testify what they have seen, and their hands have handled of the word of life—then, and not till then, will there be a general resurrection of the dry bones of the house of Israel. Amen. Lord, hasten the day!

(xxxi.) We need especially to know Christ as the "All in all." Col. iii. 11: "Where there is neither Greek nor Jew, circumcision nor uncircumcision, Barbarian, Scythian, bond nor free, but Christ is all and in all." Before the soul will cease to be overcome by temptation, it must renounce self-dependence in all things. It must be as it were self-annihilated. It must cease to think of self, as having in it any ground of dependence in the hour of trial. It must wholly and in all things renounce self, and put on Christ. It must know self as nothing in the matter of spiritual life, and Christ as all. The Psalmist could say, "All my springs are in thee." He is the fountain of life. Whatever of life is in us flows directly from him, as the sap flows from the vine to the branch; or as a rivulet flows from its fountain. The spiritual life that is in us is really Christ's life flowing through us. Our activity, though properly our own, is nevertheless stimulated and directed by his presence and agency within us. So that we can and must say with Paul, "yet not I, but Christ liveth in me." Gal. ii. 20. It is a great thing for a self-conceited sinner to suffer even in his own view, self-annihilation, as it respects the origination of any spiritual obedience to God, or any spiritual good whatever. But this must be before he will learn, on all occasions and in all things, to stand in Christ, to abide in him as his "ALL." O, the infinite folly and madness of the carnal mind! It would seem, that it will always make trial of its own strength before it will depend on Christ. It will look first for resources and help within itself, before it will renounce self, and make Christ its "all in all." It will betake itself to its own wisdom, righteousness, sanctification, and redemption. In short, there is not an office or relation of Christ, that will be recognized and embraced, until the soul has first come into circumstances to have its wants, in relation to that office of Christ, developed by some trial, and often by some fall under temptation; then, and not until, in addition to this, Christ is clearly and prevailingly revealed by the Holy Spirit, insomuch that self is put down, and Christ is exalted in the heart. Sin has so becrazed and befooled mankind, that when Christ tells them, "without me ye can do nothing," "and if any man abide not in me, he is cast forth as a branch and is withered," they neither apprehend what or how much he means, and how much is really implied in these and similar sayings, until one trial after another fully develops the appalling fact, that they are nothing, so far as spiritual good is concerned, and that Christ is "all and in all."

(xxxii.) Another relation in which the soul must know Christ, before it will steadily abide in him, is that of "the Resurrection and the Life." Through and by Christ the soul is raised from spiritual death. Christ as the resurrection and the life, is raised in the soul. He arises or revives the Divine image out of the spiritual death that reigns within us. He is begotten by the Holy Spirit, and born within us. He arises through the death that is within us, and develops his own life within our own being. Will any one say, "this is a hard saying, who can hear it?" Until we know by our own experience the power of this resurrection within us, we shall never understand "the fellowship of his sufferings and be made conformable to his death." He raises our will from its fallen state of death in trespasses and sins, or from its state of committal and voluntary enslavement to lust and to self, to a state of conformity to the will of God. Through the intellect, he pours a stream of quickening truth upon the soul. He thus quickens the will into obedience. By making fresh discoveries to the soul, he strengthens and confirms the will in obedience. By thus raising, and sustaining, and quickening the will, he rectifies the sensibility, and quickens and raises the whole man from the dead, or rather builds up a new and spiritual man upon the death and ruins of the old and carnal man. He raises the same powers and faculties that were dead in trespasses and sins to a spiritual life. He overcomes their death, and inspires them with life. He lives in saints and works in them to will and to do; and they live in him, according to the saying of Christ in his address to his Father, John xvii. 21: "As thou, Father, art in me, and I in thee, that they also may be one in us;" and again, ver. 23: "I in them and thou in me, that they may be made perfect in one." He does not raise the soul to spiritual life, in any such sense that it has life separate from him for one moment. The spiritual resurrection is a continual one. Christ is the resurrection in the sense that he is at the foundation of all our obedience at every moment. He, as it were, raises the soul or the will from the slavery of lust to a conformity to the will of God, in every instance and at every moment of its consecration to the will of God. But this he does only upon condition of our apprehending and embracing him in this relation. In reading the Bible, I have often been struck with the fact, that the inspired writers were so far ahead of the great mass of professed believers. They write of the relations in which Christ had been spiritually revealed to them. All the names, and titles, and official relations of Christ, must have had great significancy with them. They spoke not from theory, or from what man had taught them, but from experience, from what the Holy Spirit taught them. As the risen Christ is risen and lives, and is developed in one relation after another, in the experience of believers, how striking the writings of inspiration appear! As the necessities of our being are developed in experience, and as Christ is revealed, as in all new circumstances and relations, just that and all that we need, who has not marvelled to find in the Bible, way-marks, and guide-boards, and milestones, and all the evidences that we could ask or desire, that inspired men have gone this way, and have had substantially the same experiences that we have. We are often also struck with the fact, that they are so far ahead of us. At every stage in our progress we seem to have, as it were, a new and improved edition of the Bible. We discover worlds of truth before unnoticed by us—come to know Christ in precious relations in which we had known nothing of him before. And ever, as our real wants are discovered, Christ is seen to be all that we need, just the thing that exactly and fully meets the necessities of our souls. This is indeed "the glorious gospel of the blessed God."

(xxxiii.) Another precious and most influential relation of Christ in the affair of our sanctification, is that of the

Bridegroom or Husband of the soul. The individual soul needs to be espoused to Christ, to enter into this relation personally by its own consent. Mere earthly and outward marriages are nothing but sin, unless the hearts are married. True marriage is of the heart, and the outward ceremony is only a public manifestation or profession of the union or marriage of the souls or hearts. All marriage may be regarded as typical of that union into which the spiritual soul enters with Christ. This relation of Christ to the soul is frequently recognized, both in the Old and the New Testament. It is treated of by Paul as a great mystery. The seventh and eighth chapters of Romans present a striking illustration of the results of the soul's remaining under the law, on the one hand, and of its being married to Christ on the other. The seventh chapter begins thus, "Know ye not, brethren, for I speak to them that know the law, how that the law hath dominion over a man so long as he liveth. For the woman who hath a husband is bound by the law to her husband so long as he liveth; but if her husband be dead, she is loosed from the law of her husband. So then if, while her husband liveth, she be married to another man, she shall be called an adulteress; but if her husband be dead she is free from that law, so that she is no adulteress though she be married to another man. Therefore, my brethren, ye also are become dead to the law by the body of Christ: that ye should be married to another, even to Christ who is raised from the dead, that we should bring forth fruit unto God." The apostle then proceeds to show the results of these two marriages, or relations of the soul. When married to the law, he says of it, "For when we were in the flesh, the motions of sins, which were by the law, did work in our members to bring forth fruit unto death." But when married to Christ, he proceeds to say, "we are delivered from the law, that being dead wherein we were held; that we should serve in newness of spirit and not in the oldness of the letter." The remaining part of this chapter is occupied with an account of the soul's bondage while married to the law, of its efforts to please its husband, with its continual failures, its deep convictions, its selfish efforts, its consciousness of failures, and its consequent self-condemnation and despondency. It is perfectly obvious, when the allegory with which the apostle commences this chapter is considered, that he is portraying a legal experience, for the purpose of contrasting it with the experience of one who has attained to the true liberty of perfect love.

The eighth chapter represents the results of the marriage of the soul to Christ. It is delivered from its bondage to the law, and from the power of the law of sin in the members. It brings forth fruit unto God. Christ has succeeded in gaining the affections of the soul. What the law could not do Christ has done, and the righteousness of the law is now fulfilled in the soul. The representation is as follows: The soul is married to the law, and acknowledges its obligation to obey its husband. The husband requires perfect love to God and man. This love is wanting, the soul is selfish. This displeases the husband, and he denounces death against her, if she does not love. She recognizes the reasonableness of both the requisition and the threatening, and resolves upon full obedience. But being selfish, the command and threatening but increase the difficulty. All her efforts at obedience are for selfish reasons. The husband is justly firm and imperative in his demands. The wife trembles, and promises, and resolves upon obedience. But all in vain. Her obedience is only feigned, outward, and not love. She becomes disheartened and gives up in despair. As sentence is about to be executed, Christ appears. He witnesses the dilemma. He reveres, and honours, and loves the husband. He entirely approves his requisition and the course he has taken. He condemns, in most unqualified terms, the wife. Still he pities and loves her with deep benevolence. He will consent to nothing which shall have the appearance of disapproving the claims or the course of her husband. His rectitude must be openly acknowledged. Her husband must not be dishonoured.

But, on the contrary, he must be "magnified and made honourable." Still Christ so much pities the wife, as to be willing to die as her substitute. This he does, and the wife is regarded as dying in and by him her substitute. Now, since the death of either of the parties is a dissolution of the marriage covenant, and since the wife in the person of her substitute has died under and to the law her husband, she is now at liberty to marry again. Christ rises from the dead. This striking and overpowering manifestation of disinterested benevolence, on the part of Christ, in dying for her, subdues her selfishness and wins her whole heart. He proposes marriage, and she consents with her whole soul. Now she finds the law of selfishness, or of self-gratification, broken, and the righteousness of the law of love fulfilled in her heart. The last husband requires just what the first required, but having won her whole heart, she no longer needs to resolve to love, for love is as natural and spontaneous as her breath. Before the seventh of Romans was the language of her complaint. Now the eighth is the language of her triumph. Before she found herself unable to meet the demands of her husband, and equally unable to satisfy her own conscience. Now she finds it easy to obey her husband, and that his commandments are not grievous, although they are identical with those of the first husband. Now this allegory of the apostle is not a mere rhetorical flourish. It represents a reality, and one of the most important and glorious realities in existence, namely, the real spiritual union of the soul to Christ, and the blessed results of this union, the bringing forth of fruit unto God. This union is, as the apostle says, a great mystery; nevertheless, it is a glorious reality. "He that is joined unto the Lord, is one spirit." 1 Cor. vi. 17.

Now until the soul knows what it is to be married to the law, and is able to adopt the language of the seventh of Romans, it is not prepared to see, and appreciate, and be properly affected by, the death and the love of Christ. Great multitudes rest in this first marriage, and do not consent to die and rise again in Christ. They are not married to Christ, and do not know that there is such a thing, and expect to live and die in this bondage, crying out, "O wretched man that I am?" They need to die and rise again in Christ to a new life, founded in and growing out of a new relation to Christ. Christ becomes the living head or husband of the soul, its surety, its life. He gains and retains the deepest affection of the soul, thus writing his law in the heart, and engraving it in the inward parts.

But not only must the soul know what it is to be married to the law, with its consequent thraldom and death, but it must also for itself enter into the marriage relation with a risen, living Christ. This must not be a theory, an opinion, a tenet; nor must it be an imagination, a mysticism, a notion, a dream. It must be a living, personal, real entering into a personal and living union with Christ, a most entire and universal giving of self to him, and receiving of him in the relation of spiritual husband and head. The spirit of Christ and our spirit must embrace each other, and enter into an everlasting covenant with each other. There must be a mutual giving of self, and receiving of each other, a blending of spirits, in such a sense as is intended by Paul in the passage already quoted: "He that is joined to the Lord is one spirit."

My brother, my sister, do you understand this? Do you know what both these marriages are, with their diverse results? If you do not, make no longer pretence to being sanctified, for you are still in the gall of bitterness and in the bond of iniquity. "Escape for thy life."

(xxxiv.) Another interesting and highly important relation which Christ sustains to his people is that of Shepherd. This relation presupposes the helpless and defenceless condition of Christians in this life, and the indispensable necessity of guardianship and protection. Christ was revealed to the psalmist in this relation, and when on earth he revealed himself to his disciples in this relation. It is not enough, however, that he should be revealed merely in the letter, or in words as sustaining this relation. The real spiritual import of this relation, and what is implied in it, needs to be revealed by the Holy Spirit, to give it efficiency, and inspire that universal trust in the presence, care, and protection of Christ that is often essential to preventing a fall in the hour of temptation. Christ meant all that he said, when he professed to be the Good Shepherd that cared for his sheep, that would not flee, but that would lay down his life for them. In this relation, as in all others, there is infinite fulness and perfection. If the sheep do thoroughly know and confide in the shepherd, they will follow him, will flee to him for protection in every hour of danger, will at all times depend on him for all things. Now all this is received and professed in theory by all professors of religion. And yet how few, comparatively, seem to have had Christ so revealed to them, as to have secured the actual embracing of him in this relation, and a continual dependence on him for all that is implied in it. Now, either this is a vain boast of Christ, or else he may be, and ought to be depended upon, and the soul has a right to throw itself upon him for all that is implied in the relation of Good Shepherd. But this relation, with all the other relations of Christ, implies a corresponding necessity in us. This necessity we must see and feel, or this relation of Christ will have no impressive significancy. We need, then, in this case, as in all others, the revelation of the Holy Spirit, to make us thoroughly to apprehend our dependence, and to reveal Christ in the spirit and fulness of this relation, until our souls have thoroughly closed with him. Some persons fall into the mistake of supposing, that when their necessities and the fulness of Christ have been revealed to their mind by the Spirit, the work is done. But unless they actually receive him, and commit themselves to him in this relation, they will soon find to their shame that nothing has been done to purpose, so far as their standing in the hour of temptation is concerned. He may be clearly revealed in any of his relations, the soul may see both its necessities and his fulness, and yet forget or neglect actively and personally to receive him in these relations. It should never be forgotten, that this is in every case indispensable. The revelation is designed to secure our acceptance of him; if it does not do this, it has only greatly aggravated our guilt, without at all securing to us the benefits of these relations. It is amazing to see how common it is, and has been, for ministers to overlook this truth, and, of course, neither to practise it themselves, nor urge it upon their hearers. Hence Christ is not known to multitudes, and is not in many cases received even when he is revealed by the Holy Spirit. If I am not greatly mistaken, thorough inquiry would show that error upon this subject exists to a most appalling extent. The personal and individual acceptance of Christ in all his offices and relations, as the *sine quà non* of entire sanctification, seems to me to be seldom either understood or insisted on by ministers of the present day, and of course little thought of by the church. The idea of accepting for ourselves a whole Saviour, of appropriating to our own individual selves all the offices and relations of Jesus, seems to be a rare idea in this age of the church. But for what purpose does he sustain these relations? Is the bare apprehension of these truths, and of Christ in these relations enough, without our own activity being duly excited by the apprehension, to lay hold and avail ourselves of his fulness? What folly and madness for the church to expect to be saved by a neglected Saviour! To what purpose is it for the Spirit to make him known to us, unless we as individuals embrace him and make him our own? Let the soul but truly and fully apprehend and embrace Christ in this relation of Shepherd, and it shall never perish, neither shall any pluck it out of his hand. The knowing of Christ in this relation secures the soul against following strangers. But thus knowing him is indispensable to securing this result. If we know him as Shepherd we shall follow him, but not else. Let this be well considered.

(xxxv.) Christ is also the Door, by and through which the soul enters the fold, and finds security and protection among the sheep. This needs also to be spiritually apprehended, and the Door needs to be spiritually and personally entered, to secure the guardianship of the Good Shepherd. Those who do not spiritually and truly apprehend Christ as the Door, and enter by and through him, and yet hope for salvation, are surely attempting to climb up some other way, and are therefore thieves and robbers. This is a familiar and well-known truth, in the mouth, not only of every minister and Christian, but of every sabbath school child. Yet how few really apprehend and embrace its spiritual import. That there is no other means or way of access to the fold of God, is admitted by all the orthodox; but who really perceives and knows, through the personal revelation of the Holy Spirit, what, and all that Christ meant in the very significant words, "Verily, verily, I say unto you, I am the door of the sheep;" "I am the door; by me if any man enter in, he shall be saved, and shall go in and out, and find pasture?" He who truly discovers this Door, and gains access by it, will surely realize in his own experience the faithfulness of the Good Shepherd, and will go in and out, and find pasture. That is, he will surely be fed, be led into green pastures, and beside the still waters.

But it is well to inquire, what is implied in this relation of Christ.

(*a.*) It implies, that we are shut out from the protection and favour of God, except as we approach him through and by Christ.

(*b.*) It implies that we need to know, and clearly to apprehend and appreciate this fact.

(*c.*) That we need to discover the Door, and what is implied both in the Door, and in entering it.

(*d.*) That entering it implies the utter renunciation of self, of self-righteousness, self-protection and support, and a putting ourselves entirely under the control and protection of the Shepherd.

(*e.*) That we need the revelation of the Holy Spirit to make us clearly apprehend the true spiritual import of this relation, and what is implied in it.

(*f.*) That when Christ is revealed in this relation, we need to embrace him, and for ourselves to enter, by and through him, into the enclosure that everywhere surrounds the children of God.

It is an inward, and not a mere outward revelation that we need. A heart-entering revelation, and not a mere notion, idea, theory, dream of the imagination. It is really an intelligent act of the mind; as real an entering into the fold or favour of God, by and through Christ, as to enter the house of God on the sabbath-day by the door. When the soul enters by the door, it finds an infinitely different reception and treatment from that of those who climb up into the church upon a ladder of mere opinion, a scaling ladder of mere orthodoxy. This last class are not fed. They find no protection from the Good Shepherd. They do not know the Shepherd, or follow him, because they have climbed up another way. They have not confidence in him, cannot approach him with boldness, and claim his guardianship and protection. Their knowledge of Christ is but an opinion, a theory, a heartless and fruitless speculation. How many give the saddest proof that they have never entered by the door, and consequently have no realization, in their own life and experience, of the blessed and efficient protection and support of the Good Shepherd. Here I must not forget again to insist upon the necessity of a personal revelation of our relations to God, as being naturally excluded from all access to him and his favour, save through Christ the door; and also the necessity of the personal revelation to us, by the Holy Spirit, of Christ as the door, and of what is implied in this; and lastly and emphatically, upon the indispensable necessity of a personal, responsible, active, and full entering in at this door, and gaining access for ourselves to the enclosure of the love and favour of God. Let this never for one moment be forgotten or overlooked. I must enter for and by myself. I must truly enter. I must be conscious that I enter. I must be sure that I do not misapprehend what is implied on entering; and at my peril I must not forget or neglect to enter.

And here it is important to inquire, Have you had this personal and spiritual revelation? Have you clearly seen yourself without the fold, exposed to all the unrelenting cruelty of your spiritual enemies, and shut out for ever by your sin from the favour and protection of God? When this has been revealed, have you clearly apprehended Christ as the door? Have you understood what is implied in his sustaining this relation? And last, but not least, have you entered this door by faith? Have you seen the door open, and have you entered for yourself, and have you daily this evidence, that you follow the Shepherd, and find all you need?

(xxxvi.) Christ is also the Way of salvation.

Observe, he is not a mere teacher of the way, as some vainly imagine and teach. Christ is truly "the way" itself, or he is himself "the way." Works are not the way, whether these works are legal or gospel works, whether works of law or works of faith. Works of faith are a condition of salvation; but they are not "the way." Faith is not the way; faith is a condition of entering and abiding in this way, but it is not "the way." Christ is himself "the way." Faith receives him to reign in the soul, and to be its salvation; but it is Christ himself who is "the way." The soul is saved by Christ himself, not by doctrine, not by the Holy Spirit, not by works of any kind, not by faith, or love, or by anything whatever, but by Christ himself. The Holy Spirit reveals and introduces Christ to the soul, and the soul to Christ. He takes of the things of Christ and shows them to us. But he leaves it to Christ to save us. He urges and induces us to accept of Christ, to receive him by appropriating faith, as he reveals him to us. But Christ is the way. It is his being received by us, that saves the soul. But we must perceive the way; we must enter this way by our own act. We must proceed in this way. We must continue in this way to the end of life, and to all eternity, as the indispensable condition of our salvation. "Whither I go ye know, and the way ye know," said Christ. "Thomas said unto him, Lord, we know not whither thou goest, and how can we know the way?" "Jesus saith unto him, I am the way, and the truth, and the life; no man cometh unto the Father, but by me. If ye had known me ye should have known my Father also, and from henceforth ye know him, and have seen him. Philip saith unto him, Lord, show us the Father, and it sufficeth us. Jesus saith unto him, Have I been so long time with you, and yet hast thou not known me, Philip? He that hath seen me hath seen the Father, and how sayest thou then, Show us the Father? Believest thou not that I am in the Father, and the Father in me?" Here Christ so identifies himself with the Father as to insist, that he who had seen one had seen the other. When therefore he says, no man cometh to the Father but by him, we are to understand, that no man need expect to find the true God elsewhere than in him. The visible Christ embodied the true Godhead. He is the way to God, for and because he is the true God, and the eternal life, and salvation of the soul. Many seem to understand Christ in this relation as nothing more than a teacher of a system of morality, by the observance of which we may be saved. Others regard this relation as only implying, that he is the way, in the sense of making an atonement, and thus rendering it possible for us to be forgiven. Others still understand this language as implying, not only that Christ made an atonement, and opened up a way of access, through his death and mediation, to God; but also that he teaches us the great truths essential to our salvation. Now all this, in my apprehension, falls entirely, and I may say, infinitely short of the true spiritual meaning of Christ, and the true spiritual import of this relation. The above is implied and included in this relation, no doubt, but this is not all, nor the essential truth intended in Christ's declaration. He did not say, I came to open the way, nor to teach the way, nor to call you into the way, but "I am the way." Suppose he had intended merely, that his instructions pointed out the way, or that his death was to open the way, and his teaching point it out, would he not have said,—What! have I so long taught you, and have you not understood my doctrine? Would he not have said, *I have taught you the way*, instead of saying, *I am the way?* The fact is, there is a meaning in these words, more profoundly spiritual than his disciples then perceived, and than many now seem capable of understanding. He is himself the way of salvation, because he is the salvation of the soul. He is the way to the Father, because he is in the Father, and the Father in him. He is the way to eternal life, because he is himself the very essence and substance of eternal life. The soul that finds him needs not to look for eternal life, for it has found it already. These questions of Thomas and Philip show how little they really knew of Christ, previous to the baptism of the Holy Spirit. Vast multitudes of the professed disciples of the present day seem not to know Christ as "the way." They seem not to have known Christ in this relation as he is revealed by the Holy Spirit. This revelation of Christ as "the way" by the Comforter is indispensable to our so knowing him as to retain our standing in the hour of temptation. We must know, and enter, and walk, and abide in this true and living way for ourselves. It is a living way, and not a mere speculation.

Do you, my brother, know Christ by the Holy Spirit as the "living way?" Do you know Christ for yourself, by a personal acquaintance? Or do you know him only by report, by hearsay, by preaching, by reading, and by study? Do you know him as in the Father, and the Father as in him? Philip seemed not to have had a spiritual and personal revelation of the proper deity of Christ to his own soul. Have you had this revelation? And when he has been revealed to you, as the true and living way, have you by faith personally entered this way? Do you abide steadfast in it? Do you know by experience what it is to live, and move, and have your very being in God? Be ye not deceived; he that does not spiritually discern, and enter this way, and abide in it unto the end, cannot be saved. Do see to it, then, that you know the way to be sanctified, to be justified, to be saved. See to it that you do not mistake the way, and betake yourself to some other way. Remember, works are not the way. Faith is not the way. Doctrine is not the way. All these are conditions of salvation, but Christ in his own person, is "the way." His own life, living in and united to you, is the way, and the only way. You enter this way by faith; works of faith result from, and are a condition of, abiding in this way; but the way itself is the indwelling, living, personally embraced and appropriated Christ, the true God and the eternal life. Amen, Lord Jesus! the way is pleasant, and all its paths are peace.

(xxxvii.) Christ is also "the Truth," and as such he must be apprehended and embraced, to secure the soul from falling in the hour of trial. In this relation many have known Christ merely as one who declared the truth, as one who revealed the true God and the way of salvation. This is all they understand by this assertion of Christ, that he is the truth.

But if this is all, why may not the same with equal truth be said of Moses, and of Paul, and John? They taught the truth. They revealed the true God, so far as holy lives and true doctrine are concerned; and yet who ever heard of John, or Paul, or Moses, as being the way or the truth? They taught the way and the truth, but they were neither the way nor the truth, while Christ is truth. What then, is truth? Why, Christ is the truth. Whoever knows Christ spiritually knows the truth. Words are not the truth. Ideas are not the truth. Both words and ideas may be signs or representatives of the truth. But the truth lives, and has a being and a home in Christ. He is the embodiment and the essence of truth. He is reality. He is substance, and not shadow. He is truth revealed. He is elementary, essential, eternal, immutable, necessary, absolute, self-existent, infinite truth. When the Holy Spirit reveals truth, he reveals Christ. When Christ reveals truth, he reveals himself. Philosophers have found it difficult to define truth. Pilate asked Christ, "What is truth?" but did not wait for an answer. The term is doubtless used in a double sense. Sometimes the mere reflection or representation of things in signs, such as words, actions, writings, pictures, and diagrams, &c., is called truth; and this is the popular understanding of it. But all things that exist are only signs, reflections, symbols, representations, or types, of the Author of all things. That is, the universe is only the objective representation of the subjective truth, or is the reflection or reflector of God. It is the mirror that reflects the essential truth, or the true and living God.

But I am aware that none but the Holy Spirit can possess the mind of the import of this assertion of Christ. It is full of mystery and darkness, and is a mere figure of speech to one unenlightened by the Holy Spirit, in respect to its true spiritual import. The Holy Spirit does not reveal all the relations of Christ to the soul at once. Hence there are many to whom Christ has been revealed in some of his relations, while others are yet veiled from the view. Each distinct name, and office, and relation needs to be made the subject of a special and personal revelation to the soul, to meet its necessities, and to confirm it in obedience under all circumstances. When Christ is revealed and apprehended as the essential, eternal, immutable truth, and the soul has embraced him as such, as he of whom all that is popularly called truth is only the reflection, as he of whom all truth in doctrine, whether of philosophy in any of its branches, or revelation in any of its departments; I say, when the mind apprehends him as that essential truth of which all that men call truth is only the reflection, it finds a rock, a resting-place, a foundation, a stability, a reality, a power in truth, of which before it had no conception. If this is unintelligible to you, I cannot help it. The Holy Spirit can explain and make you see it; I cannot. Christ is not truth in the sense of mere doctrine, nor in the sense of a teacher of true doctrine, but as the substance or essence of truth. He is that of which all truth in doctrine treats. True doctrine treats of him, but is not identical with him. Truth in doctrine is only the sign, or declaration, or representation of truth in essence, of living, absolute, self-existent truth in the Godhead. Truth in doctrine, or true doctrine, is a medium through which substantial or essential truth is revealed. But the doctrine or medium is no more identical with truth than light is identical with the objects which it reveals. Truth in doctrine is called light, and is to essential truth what light is to the objects that radiate or reflect it. Light coming from objects is at once the condition of their revelation, and the medium through which they are revealed. So true doctrine is the condition and the means of knowing Christ the essential truth. All truth in doctrine is only a reflection of Christ, or is a radiation upon the intelligence from Christ. When we learn this spiritually, we shall learn to distinguish between doctrine and Him whose radiance it is—to worship Christ as the essential truth, and not the doctrine that reveals him—to worship God instead of the Bible. We shall then find our way through the shadow to the substance. Many, no doubt, mistake and fall down and worship the doctrine, the preacher, the Bible, the shadow, and do not look for the ineffably glorious substance, of which this bright and sparkling truth is only the sweet and mild reflection or radiation.

Dearly beloved, do not mistake the doctrine for the thing treated of by the doctrine. When you find your intellect enlightened, and your sensibility quickened by the contemplation of doctrine, do not confound this with Christ. Look steadily in the direction from which the light emanates, until the Holy Spirit enables you to apprehend the essential truth, and the true light that enlighteneth every man. Do not mistake a dim reflection of the sun for the sun himself. Do not fall down at a pool and worship the sun dimly reflected from its surface, but lift your eye and see where he stands glorious in essential, and eternal, and ineffable brightness. It is beyond question, that multitudes of professed Christians know nothing further than the doctrine of Christ; they never had Christ himself personally revealed or manifested to them. The doctrine of Christ, as taught in the gospel, is intended to direct and draw the mind to him. The soul must not rest in the doctrine, but receive the living, essential person and substance of Christ. The doctrine makes us acquainted with the facts concerning Christ, and presents him for acceptance. But do not rest in the story of Christ crucified, and risen, and standing at the door, but open the door, and receive the risen, living, and divine Saviour, as the essential and all-powerful truth to dwell within you for ever.

(xxxviii.) Christ is "the TRUE LIGHT." John says of him, "In him was life, and the life was the light of men. And the light shineth in darkness, and the darkness comprehended it not. There was a man sent from God whose name was John. The same came for a witness, to bear witness of the light, that all men through him might believe. He was not that light, but was sent to bear witness of that light. That was the TRUE LIGHT, which lighteth every man that cometh into the world." Jesus says, "I am the Light of the world; he that followeth me shall not walk in darkness, but shall have the light of life." And again, "While ye have the light, believe in the light." "I am come a light into the world." Again, it is said of Saul on his way to Damascus, "And there shined around him a light from heaven, above the brightness of the sun." It is said of Christ, in his transfiguration on the mount, "that his raiment became white as the light." Paul speaks of Christ as dwelling in light which no man can approach unto. Peter says of him, "who called you into his marvellous light." John says, "God is light, and in him is no darkness at all." Of the New Jerusalem it is said, that the inhabitants have no need of the sun, nor of the moon, "for the glory of God and the Lamb are the light thereof."

Light certainly appears to be of two kinds, as every spiritual mind knows, physical and spiritual. Physical, or natural light, reveals or makes manifest physical objects, through the fleshly organ, the eye. Spiritual light is no less real light than physical. In the presence of spiritual light the mind directly sees spiritual truths and objects, as, in the presence of material or natural light, it distinctly sees material objects. The mind has an eye, or seeing faculty, which uses the material eye and natural light, to discern material objects. It is not the eye that sees. It is always the mind that sees. It uses the eye merely as an instrument of vision, by which it discerns material objects. The eye and the light are conditions of seeing the material universe, but it is always the mind that sees. So the mind directly sees spiritual realities in the presence of spiritual light. But what is light? What is natural, and what is spiritual light? Are they really identical, or are they essentially different? It is not my purpose here to enter into any philosophical speculations upon this subject; but I must observe, that, whatever spiritual light is, the mind, under certain circumstances, cannot discern the difference, if difference there is, between them. Was that spiritual or physical light which the disciples saw on the mount of transfiguration? Was that spiritual or physical light which Paul and his companions saw on their way to Damascus? What light is that which falls upon the mental eye of the believer when he draws so near to God, as not at all to distinguish at the moment the glory that surrounds him from material light? What was that light which made the face of Moses shine with such brightness, that the people were unable to look upon it? And what is that light which lights up the countenance of a believer, when he comes direct and fresh from the mount of communion with God? There is often a visible light in his countenance. What is that light which often shines upon the pages of the Bible, making its spiritual meaning as manifest to the mind, as the letters and words are? In such seasons the obscurity is removed from the spirit of the Bible, just as really and as visibly, as the rising sun would remove the obscurity of midnight from the letter. In one case you perceive the letter clearly in the presence of natural light. You have no doubt, you can have no doubt, that you see the letters and words as they are. In the other, you apprehend the spirit of the Bible, just as clearly as you see the letter. You can no more doubt, at the time, that you see the true spiritual import of the words, than that you see the words themselves. Both the letter and the spirit seem to be set in so strong a light, that you know that you see both. Now what light is this in which the spirit of the Bible is seen? That it is light, every spiritual man knows. He calls it light. He can call it nothing else. At other times the letter is as distinctly visible as before, and yet there is no possibility of discerning the spirit of the Bible. It is then only known in the letter. We are then left to philologize, and philosophize, and theorize, and theologize, and are really all in the dark, as to the true spiritual import of the Bible. But when "the true light that lighteth every man" shines upon the word, we get at once a deeper insight into the real spiritual import of the word, than we could have gotten in a life-time without it. Indeed, the true spiritual import of the Bible is hid from the learning of this world, and revealed to the babes who are in the light of Christ. I have often been afflicted with the fact, that true spiritual light is rejected and condemned, and the very idea of its existence scouted by many men who are wise in the wisdom of this world. But the Bible everywhere abounds with evidence, that spiritual light exists, and that its presence is a condition of apprehending the reality and presence of spiritual objects. It has been generally supposed, that the natural sun is the source of natural light. Sure it is, that light is a condition of our beholding the objects of the material universe. But what is the source of spiritual light? The Bible says Christ is. But what does this mean? When it is said, that he is the true light, does it mean only, that he is the teacher of true doctrine? or does it mean, that he is the light in which true doctrine is apprehended, or its spiritual import understood, that he shines through and upon all spiritual doctrine, and causes its spiritual import to be apprehended, and that the presence of his light, or, in other words, his own presence, is a condition of any doctrine being spiritually understood? He is no doubt the essential light. That is, light is an attribute of his divinity. Essential, uncreated light is one of the attributes of Christ as God. It is a spiritual attribute of course; but it is an essential and a natural attribute of Christ, and whoever knows Christ after the Spirit, or whoever has a true, spiritual, and personal acquaintance with Christ as God, knows that Christ is light, that his being called light is not a mere figure of speech; that his "covering himself with light as with a garment;" his enlightening the heavenly world with so ineffable a light, that no man can approach thereunto and live, that the strongest seraphim are unable to look with unveiled face upon his overpowering effulgence. I say, to a spiritual mind these are not mere figures of speech; they are understood by those who walk in the light, or who walk in the light of Christ, to mean what they say.

I dwell upon this particular relation of Christ, because of the importance of its being understood, that Christ is the real and true light who alone can cause us to see spiritual things as they are. Without his light we walk in the midst of the most overpowering realities, without being at all aware of their presence. Like one surrounded with natural darkness, or as one deprived of sight gropes his way and knows not at what he stumbles, so one deprived of the presence and light of Christ, gropes his way and stumbles at he knows not what. To attain to true spiritual illumination, and to continue and walk in this light, is indispensable to entire sanctification. O, that this were understood! Christ must be known as the true and only light of the soul. This must not be held merely as a tenet. It must be understood and spiritually experienced and known. That Christ is in some undeterminate sense the light of the soul and the true light, is generally admitted, just as multitudes of other things are admitted, without being at all spiritually and experimentally understood. But this relation or attribute of Christ must be spiritually known by experience, as a condition of abiding in him. John says, "this then is the message which we have heard of him, that God is light, and in him is no darkness at all. If we say that we have fellowship with him, and walk in darkness, we lie and do not the truth. But if we walk in the light as he is in the light, we have fellowship one with another, and the blood of Jesus Christ his Son cleanseth us from all sin." This light is come into the world, and if men do not love darkness rather than light, they will know Christ as the true light of the soul, and will so walk in the light as not to stumble.

I desire much to amplify upon this relation of Christ, but must forbear, or I shall too much enlarge this course of instruction. I would only endeavour to impress you deeply with the conviction that Christ is light, and that this is no figure of speech. Rest not, my brother, until you truly and experimentally know him as such. Bathe your soul daily in his light, so that when you come from your closet to your pulpit, your people shall behold your face shining as if it were the face of an angel.

(xxxix.) Another relation which Christ sustains to the believer, and which it is indispensable that he should recognize and spiritually apprehend, as a condition of entire sanctification, is that of "Christ within us."

"Know ye not," says the apostle, "that Jesus Christ is in you, except ye be reprobates."—2 Cor. xiii. 5. "But ye are not in the flesh, but in the Spirit, if the Spirit of God dwell in you. Now if any man have not the Spirit of Christ, he is none of his. And if Christ be in you, the body is dead because of sin, but the Spirit is life because of righteousness."—Rom. viii. 9, 10. "My little children, of whom I travail in birth again until Christ be formed in you."—Gal. iv. 19. "Yet not I but Christ liveth in me."—Gal. ii. 20. Now it has often appeared to me, that many know Christ only as an outward Christ, as one who lived many hundred years ago, who died, and arose, and ascended on high, and who now lives in heaven. They read all this in the Bible, and in a certain sense they believe it. That is, they admit it to be true historically. But have they Christ risen within them? Living within the veil of their own flesh, and there ever making intercession for them and in them? This is quite another thing. Christ in heaven making intercession is one thing; this is a great and glorious truth. But Christ in the soul, there also living "to make intercession for us with groanings that cannot be uttered," is another thing. The Spirit that dwells in the saints is frequently in the Bible represented as the Spirit of Christ, and as Christ himself. Thus in the passage just quoted from the eighth of Romans, the apostle represents the Spirit of God that dwells in the saints as the Spirit of Christ, and as Christ himself.—Rom. viii. 9, 10: "But ye are not in the flesh, but in the Spirit, if so be that the Spirit of God dwell in you. Now if any man have not the Spirit of Christ, he is none of his. And if Christ be in you, the body is dead because of sin; but the Spirit is life because of righteousness." This is common in the Bible. The Spirit of Christ then, or the real Deity of Christ, dwells in the truly spiritual believer. But this fact needs to be spiritually apprehended, and kept distinctly and continually in view. Christ not only in heaven, but Christ within us, as really and truly inhabiting our bodies as we do, as really in us as we are in ourselves, is the teaching of the Bible, and must be spiritually apprehended by a divine, personal, and inward revelation, to secure our abiding in him. We not only need the real presence of Christ within us, but we need his manifested presence to sustain us in hours of conflict. Christ may be really present within us as he is without us, without our apprehending his presence. His manifesting himself to us as with and in us, is by himself conditionated upon our faith and obedience. His manifesting himself within us, and thus assuring us of his constant and real presence, confirms and establishes the confidence and obedience of the soul. To know Christ after the flesh, or merely historically as an outward Saviour, is of no spiritual avail. We must know him as an inward Saviour, as Jesus risen and reigning in us, as having arisen and established his throne in our hearts, and as having written and established the authority of his law there. The old man dethroned and crucified, Christ risen within us and united to us, in such a sense that we "twain are one spirit," is the true and only condition and secret of entire sanctification. O that this were understood! Why, many ministers talk and write about sanctification, just as if they supposed, that it consisted in, and resulted from, a mere self-originated formation of holy habits. What blindness is this in spiritual guides! True sanctification consists in entire consecration to God; but be it ever remembered, that this consecration is induced and perpetuated by the Spirit of Christ. The fact, that Christ is in us, needs to be so clearly apprehended by us as to annihilate the conception of Christ as only afar off, in heaven. The soul needs so to apprehend this truth, as to turn within, and not look without for Christ, so that it will naturally seek communion with him in the closet of the soul, or within, and not let the thoughts go in search of him without. Christ promised to come and take up his abode with his people, to manifest himself unto them, &c., that the Spirit whom he would send, (which was his own Spirit, as abundantly appears from the Bible,) should abide with them for ever, that he should be with them and in them. Now all this language needs to be spiritually apprehended, and Christ needs to be recognized by his Spirit, as really present with us as we are with ourselves, and really as near to us as we are to ourselves, and as infinitely more interested in us than we are in ourselves. This spiritual recognition of Christ present with and in us, has an overpowering charm in it. The soul rests in him, and lives, and walks, and has its being in his light, and drinks at the fountain of his love. It drinks also of the river of his pleasures. It enjoys his peace, and leans upon his strength.

Many professors have not Christ formed within them. The Galatian Christians had fallen from Christ. Hence the apostle says: "My little children, of whom I travail in birth again until Christ be formed in you." Have you a spiritual apprehension of what this means?

(xl.) We must spiritually know Christ as "our strength," as a condition of entire sanctification. Says the Psalmist, Ps. xviii. 1: "I will love thee, O Lord, my strength;" and again, Ps. xix. 14: "O Lord my strength;" and again, Ps. xxxi. 4: "Pull me out of the net, for thou art my strength;" and again, Ps. xliii. 2: "Thou art the God of my strength:" and again, Ps. lix. 17: "To thee, O my strength, will I sing;" and again, Ps. cxliv. 1: "Blessed be the Lord my strength." In Is. xxvii. 5: "The Lord says, Let him take hold of my strength, and he shall make peace with me." Jeremiah says, ch. xvi. 19: "O Lord, my strength." Hab. iii. 9: "God is my strength." In 2 Cor. xii. 9, Christ says to Paul, "My strength is made perfect in weakness." We are commanded to be strong in the Lord, and in the power of his might, that is, to appropriate his strength by faith. We are exhorted to take hold of his strength, and doing this is made a condition of making peace with God. That God is in some sense our strength, is generally admitted. But I fear it is rare to apprehend the true spiritual sense in which he is our strength. Many take refuge not in his strength by faith, but in the plea, that he is their strength, and that they have none of their own, while they continue in sin. But this class of persons neither truly understand nor believe, that God is their strength. It is with all who hold this language and yet live in sin, an opinion, a tenet, a say-so, but by no means a spiritually apprehended and embraced truth. If the real meaning of this language were spiritually apprehended and embraced with the heart, the soul would no more live in sin. It could no more be overcome with temptation, while appropriating Christ, than God could be overcome.

The conditions of spiritually apprehending Christ as our strength are,—

(*a*.) The spiritual apprehension of our own weakness, its nature and degree.

(*b*.) The revelation of Christ to us as our strength by the Holy Spirit.

When these revelations are truly made, and self-dependence is, therefore, for ever annihilated, the soul comes to understand wherein its strength lies. It renounces for ever its own strength, and relies wholly on the strength of Christ. This it does not in the antinomian, do-nothing, sit-still sense of the term; but, on the contrary, it actively takes hold of Christ's strength, and uses it in doing all the will of God. It does not sit down and do nothing, but, on the contrary, it takes hold of Christ's strength, and sets about every good word and work as one might lean upon the strength of another, and go about doing good. The soul that understands and does this, as really holds on to and leans upon Christ, as a helpless man would lean upon the arm or shoulder of a strong man, to be borne about in some benevolent enterprise. It is not a state of quietism. It is not a mere opinion, a sentiment, a fancy. It is, with the sanctified soul, one of the clearest realities in existence, that he leans upon and uses the strength of Christ. He knows himself to be constantly and perseveringly active, in thus availing himself of the strength of Christ; and being perfectly weak in himself, or perfectly emptied of his own strength, Christ's strength is made perfect in his weakness. This renunciation of his own strength is not a denial of his natural ability, in any such sense as virtually to charge God with requiring what he is unable to perform. It is a complete recognition of his ability, were he disposed to do all that God requires of him, and implies a thorough and honest condemnation of himself for not using his powers as God requires. But while it recognizes its natural liberty or ability, and its consequent obligation, it at the same time clearly and spiritually sees, that it has been too long the slave of lust ever to assert or to maintain its spiritual supremacy, as the master instead of the slave of appetite. It sees so clearly and affectingly, that the will or heart is so weak in the presence of temptation, that there is no hope of its maintaining its integrity, unsupported by strength from Christ, that it renounces for ever its dependence on its own strength, and casts itself wholly and for ever on the strength of Christ. Christ's strength is appropriated only upon condition of a full renunciation of one's own. And Christ's strength is made perfect in the soul of man only in its entire weakness; that is, only in the absence of all dependence on its own strength. Self must be renounced in every respect in which we appropriate Christ. He will not share the throne of the heart with us, nor will he be put on by us, except in so far as we put off ourselves. Lay aside all dependence on yourself, in every respect in which you would have Christ. Many reject Christ by depending on self, and seem not to be aware of their error.

Now, let it be understood and constantly borne in mind, that this self-renunciation and taking hold on Christ as our strength, is not a mere speculation, an opinion, an article of faith, a profession, but must be one of the most practical realities in the world. It must become to the mind an omnipresent reality, insomuch that you shall no more attempt any thing in your own strength than a man who never could walk without crutches would attempt to arise and walk without thinking of them. To such a one his crutches become a part of himself. They are his legs. He as naturally uses them as we do the members of our body. He no more forgets them, or attempts to walk without them, than we attempt to walk without our feet. Now just so it is with one who spiritually understands his dependence on Christ. He knows he can walk, and that he must walk, but he as naturally uses the strength of Christ in all his duties, as the lame man uses his crutches. It is as really an omnipresent reality to him, that he must lean upon Christ, as it is to the lame man that he must lean upon his crutch. He learns on all occasions to keep hold of the strength of Christ, and does not even think of doing any thing without him. He knows that he need not attempt any thing in his own strength; and that if he should, it will result in failure and disgrace, just as really and as well as the man without feet or legs knows that for him to attempt to walk without his crutch would ensure a fall. This is a great, and, I fear, a rarely learned lesson with professed Christians, and yet how strange that it should be so, since, in every instance, attempts to walk without Christ have resulted in complete and instantaneous failure. All profess to know their own weakness and their remedy, and yet how few give evidence of knowing either.

(xli.) Christ is also the Keeper of the soul; and in this relation he must be revealed to, and embraced by, each soul as the condition of its abiding in Christ, or, which is the same thing, as a condition of entire sanctification. Ps. cxxi. "I will lift up mine eyes unto the hills, from whence cometh my help. My help cometh from the Lord, which made heaven and earth. He will not suffer thy foot to be moved; he that keepeth thee will not slumber. Behold he that keepeth Israel shall neither slumber nor sleep. The Lord is thy keeper; the Lord is thy shade upon thy right hand. The sun shall not smite thee by day, nor the moon by night. The Lord shall preserve thee from all evil; he shall preserve thy soul. The Lord shall preserve thy going out, and thy coming in, from this time forth, and even for evermore." This Psalm, with a great many other passages of scripture, represents God as exerting an efficient influence in preserving the soul from falling. This influence he exerts, of course not physically or by compulsion, but it is and must be a moral influence, that is, an influence entirely consistent with our own free agency. But it is efficient in the sense of being a prevailing influence.

But in this relation, as in all others, Christ must be apprehended and embraced. The soul must see and well appreciate its dependence in this respect, and commit itself to Christ in this relation. It must cease from its own works, and from expecting to keep itself, and commit itself to Christ, and abide in this state of committal. Keeping the soul implies watching over it to guard it against being overcome with temptation. This is exactly what the Christian needs. His enemies are the world, the flesh, and Satan. By these he has been enslaved. To them he has been consecrated. In their presence he is all weakness in himself. He needs a keeper to accompany him, just as a reformed inebriate sometimes needs one to accompany and strengthen him in scenes of temptation. The long established habitudes of the drunkard render him weak in the presence of his enemy, the intoxicating bowl. So the Christian's long-cherished habits of self-indulgence render him all weakness and irresolution, if left to himself in the presence of excited appetite or passion. As the inebriate needs a friend and brother to warn and expostulate, to suggest considerations to strengthen his purposes, so the sinner needs the Parakletos to warn and suggest considerations to sustain his fainting resolutions. This Christ has promised to do; but this, like all the promises, is conditionated upon our appropriating it to our own use by faith. Let it then be ever borne in mind, that as our keeper, the Lord must be spiritually apprehended and cordially embraced and depended upon, as a condition of entire sanctification. This must not be a mere opinion. It must be a thorough and honest closing in with Christ in this relation.

Brother, do you know what it is to depend on Christ in this relation, in such a sense, that you as naturally hold fast to him, as a child would cling to the hand or the neck of a father, when in the midst of perceived danger? Have you seen your need of a keeper? If so, have you fled to Christ in this relation? As ye have received Christ Jesus the Lord, so walk ye in him, that is, abide in him, and he will abide in you, and keep you from falling. The apostle certifies, or rather assumes, that he is able to keep you from falling. "Now unto Him that is able to keep you from falling, and to present you faultless before the presence of his glory with exceeding joy—to the only wise God, our Saviour, be glory and majesty, dominion and power, both now and ever. Amen."—Jude 24, 25. Paul also says: "I know in whom I have believed, and am persuaded that he is able to keep that which I have committed to him against that day."

(xlii.) The soul also needs to know Christ, not merely as a master, but as a Friend. John xv. 13-15: "Greater love hath no man than this, that a man lay down his life for his friends. Ye are my friends, if ye do whatsoever I command you. Henceforth I call you not servants, for the servant knoweth not what his lord doeth; but I have called you friends, for all things that I have heard of my Father I have made known unto you."

Christ took the utmost pains to inspire his disciples with the most implicit confidence in himself. He does the same still. Most Christians seem not to have apprehended the condescension of Christ sufficiently to appreciate fully, not to say at all, his most sincere regard for them. They seem afraid to regard him in the light of a friend, one whom they may approach on all occasions with the utmost confidence and holy familiarity, one who takes a lively interest in everything that concerns them, one who sympathizes with them in all their trials, and feels more tenderly for them than they do for their nearest earthly friends. Observe, what emphasis he gives to this relation, or to the strength of his friendship. He lays down his life for his friends. Now, imagine yourself to have an earthly friend who loved you so much as to lay down his life for you; to die too for a crime which you had committed against himself. Were you assured of the strength of his friendship, and did you know withal his ability to help you in all circumstances to be absolutely unlimited, with what confidence would you unbosom yourself to him! How would you rest in his friendship and protection! How slow even Christians are to apprehend Christ in the relation of a friend. They stand in so much awe of him, that they fear to take home to their hearts the full import and reality of the relation when applied to Christ. Yet Christ takes the greatest pains to inspire them with the fullest confidence in his undying and most exalted friendship.

I have often thought that many professed Christians had never really and spiritually apprehended Christ in this relation. This accounts for their depending upon him so little in seasons of trial. They do not realize that he truly feels for and sympathizes with them, that is, his feeling for and sympathy with them, his deep interest in and pity for them, are not apprehended spiritually as a reality. Hence they stand aloof, or approach him only in words, or at most, with deep feeling and desire, but not in the unwavering confidence that they shall receive the things which they ask of him. But to prevail they must believe. "For he that wavereth is like a wave of the sea, driven with the wind and tossed. For let not that man think that he shall receive anything of the Lord." The real, and deep, and abiding affection of Christ for us, and his undying interest in us personally, must come to be a living and an omnipresent reality to our souls, to secure our own abiding in faith and love in all circumstances. There is, perhaps, no relation of Christ in which we need more thoroughly to know him than this.

This relation is admitted in words by almost everybody, yet duly realized and believed by almost nobody. Yet how infinitely strange, that Christ should have given so high evidence of his love to, and friendship for us, and that we should be so slow of heart to believe and realize it! But until this truth is really and spiritually apprehended and embraced, the soul will find it impossible to fly to him in seasons of trial, with implicit confidence in his favour and protection. But let Christ be really apprehended and embraced, as a friend who has laid down his life for us, and would not hesitate to do it again were it needful, and rely upon it, our confidence in him will secure our abiding in him.

(xliii.) Christ is also to be regarded and embraced in the relation of an Elder Brother. Heb. ii. 10-18: "For it became him, for whom are all things, and by whom are all things, in bringing many sons unto glory, to make the Captain of their salvation perfect through sufferings. For both he that sanctifieth and they who are sanctified are all of one, for which cause he is not ashamed to call them brethren; saying, I will declare thy name unto my brethren; in the midst of the church will I sing praise unto thee. And again, I will put my trust in him. And again, Behold I, and the children which God hath given me. Forasmuch then as the children are partakers of flesh and blood, he also himself likewise took part of the same: that through death he might destroy him that had the power of death, that is, the devil; and deliver them who through fear of death were all their lifetime subject to bondage. For verily he took not on him the nature of angels; but he took on him the seed of Abraham. Wherefore in all things it behoved him to be made like unto his brethren, that he might be a merciful and faithful high priest in things pertaining to God, to make reconciliation for the sins of the people: for in that he himself hath suffered, being tempted, he is able to succour them that are tempted." Matt. xxviii. 10: "Then said Jesus unto them, Be not afraid: go tell my brethren, that they go into Galilee, and there shall they see me." John xx. 17: "Jesus saith unto her, Touch me not; for I am not yet ascended to my Father: but go to my brethren, and say unto them, I ascend unto my Father, and your Father; and to my God, and your God." Rom. viii. 29: "For whom he did foreknow, he also did predestinate to be conformed to the image of his Son, that he might be the first-born among many brethren." These and other passages present Christ in the relation of a brother. So he is not merely a friend, but a brother. He is a brother possessing the attributes of God. And is it not of great importance, that in this relation we should know and embrace him? It would seem as if all possible pains were taken by him to inspire us with the most implicit confidence in him. He is not ashamed to call us brethren; and shall we refuse or neglect to embrace him in this relation, and avail ourselves of all that is implied in it? I have often thought that many professed Christians really regard the relations of Christ as only existing in name, and not at all in reality and fact. Am I not a man and a brother? he says to the desponding and tempted soul. Himself hath said, A brother is made for adversity. He is the first-born among many brethren, and yet we are to be heirs with him, heirs of God, and joint heirs with him of all the infinite riches of the Godhead. "O fools and slow of heart," not to believe and receive this brother to our most implicit and eternal confidence. He must be spiritually revealed, apprehended, and embraced in this relation, as a condition of our experiencing his fraternal truthfulness.

Do let me inquire whether many Christians do not regard such language as pathetic and touching, but after all as only a figure of speech, as a pretence, rather than as a serious and infinitely important fact. Is the Father really our Father? Then Christ is our Brother, not in a figurative sense merely, but literally and truly our brother. My brother? Ah truly, and a brother made for adversity. O Lord, reveal thyself fully to our souls in this relation!

(xliv.) Christ is the true Vine, and we are the branches. And do we know him in this relation, as our parent stock, as the fountain from whom we receive our momentary nourishment and life? This union between Christ and our souls is formed by implicit faith in him. By faith the soul leans on him, feeds upon him, and receives a constantly sustaining influence from him. John xv. 1-8: "I am the true vine, and my

Father is the husbandman. Every branch in me that beareth not fruit he taketh away; and every branch that beareth fruit he purgeth it, that it may bring forth more fruit. Now ye are clean through the word which I have spoken unto you. Abide in me, and I in you. As the branch cannot bear fruit of itself, except it abide in the vine; no more can ye, except ye abide in me. I am the vine, ye are the branches: he that abideth in me, and I in him, the same bringeth forth much fruit; for without me ye can do nothing. If a man abide not in me, he is cast forth as a branch, and is withered; and men gather them, and cast them into the fire, and they are burned. If ye abide in me, and my words abide in you, ye shall ask what ye will, and it shall be done unto you. Herein is my Father glorified, that ye bear much fruit; so shall ye be my disciples." Now, it is important for us to understand what it is to be in Christ, in the sense of this passage. It certainly is to be so united to him, as to receive as real and as constant spiritual support and nourishment from him, as the branch does natural nourishment from the vine. "If a man abide not in me," he says, "he is cast forth as a branch and is withered." Now, to be in him, implies such a union as to keep us spiritually alive and fresh. There are many withered professors in the church. They abide not in Christ. Their religion is stale. They can speak of former experience. They can tell how they once knew Christ, but every spiritual mind can see, that they are branches fallen off. They have no fruit. Their leaves are withered, their bark is dried; and they are just fit to be gathered and cast into the fire. O, this stale, last year's religion! Why will not professors that live on an old experience, understand that they are cast off branches, and that their withered, fruitless, lifeless, loveless, faithless, powerless condition testifies to their faces, and before all men, that they are fit fuel for the flames?

It is also of infinite importance, that we should know and spiritually apprehend the conditions of abiding in Christ, in the relation of a branch to a vine. We must apprehend our various necessities and his infinite fulness, and lay hold upon, and appropriate the whole that is implied in these relations, to our own souls and wants, as fast as he is revealed. Thus we shall abide in him, and receive all the spiritual nourishment we need. But unless we are thus taught by the Spirit, and unless we thus believe, we shall not abide in him, nor he in us. If we do thus abide in him, he says, we shall bear much fruit. Much fruit then is evidence that we do abide in him, and fruitlessness is positive evidence that we do not abide in him. "If ye abide in me, and my words abide in you, ye shall ask what ye will, and it shall be done unto you." Great prevalence in prayer, then, is an evidence that we abide in him. But a want of prevalence in prayer is conclusive evidence that we do not abide in him. No man sins while he properly abides in Christ. "If any man be in Christ, he is a new creature. Old things are passed away, and behold all things are become new."

But let it not be forgotten that we have something to do to abide in Christ. "Abide in me," says Christ: this is required of us. We neither at first come to sustain the relation of a branch to Christ without our own activity, nor do or can we abide in him without a constant cleaving to him by faith. The will must of necessity be ever active. It must cleave to Christ or to something else. It is one thing to hold this relation in theory, and an infinitely different thing to understand it spiritually, and really cleave to Christ in the relation of the constant fountain of spiritual life.

(xlv.) Christ is also the "Fountain opened in the house of David for sin and uncleanness;"—Zec. xiii. 1. Christ, let it be ever remembered, and spiritually understood and embraced, is not only a justifying, but also a purifying Saviour. His name is Jesus, because he saves his people from their sins.

(xlvi.) As Jesus, therefore, he must be spiritually known and embraced. Jesus, Saviour! He is called Jesus, or Saviour, we are informed, because he saves his people, not only from hell, but also from their sins. He saves from hell only upon condition of his saving from sin. He has no Saviour, who is not in his own experience saved from sin. Of what use is it to call Jesus, Lord and Saviour, unless he is really and practically acknowledged as our Lord and as our Saviour from sin? Shall we call him Lord, Lord, and do not the things which he says? Shall we call him Saviour, and refuse so to embrace him as to be saved from our sins?

(xlvii.) We must know him as one whose blood cleanses us from all sin. Heb. ix. 14.—"How much more shall the blood of Christ, who through the eternal Spirit offered himself without spot to God, purge your conscience from dead works to serve the living God!" 1 Peter i. 19.—"But with the precious blood of Christ, as of a lamb without blemish and without spot." 1 Peter i. 2.—"Elect according to the foreknowledge of God the Father, through sanctification of the Spirit, unto obedience and sprinkling of the blood of Jesus Christ." Rev. i. 5.—"Unto him that loved us, and washed us from our sins in his own blood." When the shedding of Christ's blood is rightly apprehended and embraced, when his atonement is properly understood and received by faith, it cleanses the soul from all sin; or rather, I should say, that when Christ is received as one to cleanse us from sin by his blood, we shall know what James B. Taylor meant when he said, "I have been into the fountain, and am clean;" and what Christ meant when he said, "Now ye are clean through the word which I have spoken unto you." "Who hath loved us, and washed us from our sins in his own blood." "Then will I sprinkle clean water upon you and ye shall be clean, from all your filthiness and from all your idols will I cleanse you. A new heart also will I give you, and a new spirit will I put within you. I will take away the stony heart out of your flesh, and give you a heart of flesh." It is of the last importance that language like this, relating to our being cleansed from sin by Christ, should be elucidated to our souls by the Holy Spirit, and embraced by faith, and Christ truly revealed in this relation. Nothing but this can save us from sin. But this will fully and effectually do the work. It will cleanse us from all sin. It will cleanse us from all our filthiness, and from all our idols. It will make us "clean."

(xlviii.) "His name shall be called Wonderful." No inward or audible exclamation is more common to me of late years, than the term Wonderful. When contemplating the nature, the character, the offices, the relations, the salvation of Christ, I find myself often mentally, and frequently audibly exclaiming, WONDERFUL! My soul is filled with wonder, love, and praise, as I am led by the Holy Spirit to apprehend Christ, sometimes in one and sometimes in another relation, as circumstances and trials develope the need I have of him. I am more and more "astonished at the doctrine of the Lord," and at the Lord himself from year to year. I have come to the conclusion, that there is no end to this, either in time or in eternity. He will no doubt to all eternity continue to make discoveries of himself to his intelligent creatures, that shall cause them to exclaim "WONDERFUL!" I find my wonder more and more excited from one stage of Christian experience to another. Christ is indeed wonderful, contemplated in every point of view, as God, as man, as God-man, mediator. Indeed, I hardly know in which of his many relations he appears most wonderful, when in that relation he is revealed by the Holy Spirit. All, all is wonderful, when he stands revealed to the soul in any of his relations. The soul needs to be so acquainted with him as to excite and constantly keep awake its wonder and adoration. Contemplate Christ in any point of view, and the wonder of the soul is excited. Look at any feature of his character, at any department of the plan of salvation, at any part that he takes in the glorious work of man's redemption; look steadfastly at him as he is revealed through the gospel by the Holy Spirit, at any time and place, in any of his works or ways, and the soul will instantly exclaim—WONDERFUL! Yes, he shall be called Wonderful!

(xlix.) "Counsellor." Who that has made Jesus his wisdom, does not and has not often recognized the fitness of calling him "Counsellor?" Until he is known and embraced in this relation, it is not natural or possible for the soul to go to him with implicit confidence in every case of doubt. Almost everybody holds in theory the propriety and necessity of consulting Christ, in respect to the affairs that concern ourselves and his church. But it is one thing to hold this opinion, and quite another to apprehend and embrace Christ so spiritually in the relation of counsellor, as naturally to call him counsellor when approaching him in secret, and as naturally to turn and consult him on all occasions and in respect to everything that concerns us; and to consult him too with implicit confidence in his ability and willingness to give us the direction we need. Thoroughly and spiritually to know Christ in this relation is undoubtedly a condition of abiding steadfast in him. Unless the soul knows and duly appreciates its dependence upon him in this relation, and unless it renounces its own wisdom, and substitutes his in the place of it, by laying hold of Christ by faith as the counsellor of the soul, it will not continue to walk in his counsel, and consequently will not abide in his love.

(l.) The Mighty God. "My Lord and my God," exclaimed Thomas, when Christ stood spiritually revealed to him. It was not merely what Christ said to Thomas on that occasion, that caused him to utter the exclamation just quoted. Thomas saw indeed that Christ was raised from the dead, but so had Lazarus been raised from the dead. The mere fact, therefore, that Christ stood before him as one raised from the dead, could not have been proof that he was God. No doubt the Holy Spirit discovered to Thomas at the moment the true Divinity of Christ, just as the saints in all ages have had him spiritually revealed to them as the Mighty God. I have long been convinced, that it is in vain, so far as any spiritual benefit is concerned, to attempt to convince Unitarians of the proper

Divinity of Christ. The scriptures are as plain as they can be upon this subject, and yet it is true, that no man can say that Jesus is the Lord but by the Holy Spirit. As I have said in substance often, the personal revelation of Christ to the inward man by the Holy Spirit, is a condition of his being known as the "Mighty God." What is Christ to any one who does not know him as God? To such a soul, he cannot be a Saviour. It is impossible that the soul should intelligently, and without idolatry, commit itself to him as a Saviour, unless it knows him to be the true God. It cannot innocently pray to him nor worship him, nor commit the soul to his keeping and protection, until it knows him as the Mighty God. To be orthodox merely in theory, in opinion, is nothing to the purpose of salvation. The soul must know Christ as God—must believe in or receive him as such. To receive him as anything else is an infinitely different thing from coming and submitting to him as the true, and living, and mighty God.

(li.) Christ is our Shield. By this name, or in this relation, he has always been known to the saints. God said to Abraham, "I am thy shield."—Gen. xv. 1. Ps. xxxiii. 20: "The Lord is my shield." Prov. xxx. 5: "He is a shield to them that put their trust in him." A shield is a piece of defensive armour used in war. It is a broad plate made of wood or metal, and borne upon the arm and hand, and in conflict presented between the body and the enemy to protect it against his arrows or his blows. God is the Christian's shield in the spiritual warfare. This is a most interesting and important relation. He who does not know Christ in this relation, and has not embraced and put him on, as one would buckle on a shield, is all exposed to the assaults of the enemy, and will surely be wounded if not slain by his fiery darts. This is more than a figure of speech. No fact or reality is of more importance to the Christian, than to know how to hide himself behind and in Christ in the hour of conflict. Unless the Christian has on his shield, and knows how to use it, he will surely fall in battle. When Satan appears, the soul must present its shield, must take refuge behind and in Christ, or all will be defeat and disgrace. When faith presents Christ as the shield, Satan retires vanquished from the field in every instance. Christ always makes way for our escape; and never did a soul get wounded in conflict who made the proper use of this shield. But Christ needs to be known as our protection, as ready on all occasions to shield us from the curse of the law, and from the artillery of the enemy of our souls. Be sure to truly know him, and put him on in this relation, and then you may always sing of victory.

(lii.) The Lord is "the Portion" of his people. "I am thy shield and thy exceeding great reward," said God to Abraham. As the reward or portion of the soul, we need to know and embrace Christ as the condition of abiding in him. We need to know him as "our exceeding great portion,"—a present, all-satisfying portion. Unless we so know Christ as to be satisfied with him, as all we can ask or desire, we shall not of course abstain from all forbidden sources of enjoyment. Nothing is more indispensable to our entire sanctification, than to apprehend the fulness there is in Christ in this relation. When the soul finds in him all its desires and all its wants fully met, when it sees in him all that it can conceive of as excellent and desirable, and that he is its portion, it remains at rest. It has little temptation to go after other lovers, or after other sources of enjoyment. It is full. It has enough. It has an infinitely rich and glorious inheritance. What more can it ask or think? The soul that understands what it is to have Christ as its portion, knows that he is an infinite portion; that eternity can never exhaust, or even diminish it in the least degree; that the mind shall to all eternity increase in the capacity of enjoying this portion; but that no increase of capacity and enjoyment can diminish ought of the infinite fulness of the Divine Portion of our souls.

(liii.) Christ is our Hope. 1 Tim. i. 1: "Paul, an apostle of Jesus Christ, by the commandment of God our Saviour, and Lord Jesus Christ, which is our hope." Col. i. 27: "To whom God would make known what is the riches of the glory of this mystery among the gentiles; which is Christ in you the hope of glory." Our only rational expectation is from him. Christ in us is our hope of glory. Without Christ in us we have no good or well-grounded hope of glory. Christ in the gospel, Christ on the cross, Christ risen, Christ in heaven, is not our hope; but Christ in us, Christ actually present, living, and reigning in us, as really as he lives and reigns in glory, is our only well-grounded hope. We cannot be too certain of this, for unless we despair of salvation in ourselves or in any other, we do not truly make Christ our hope. The soul that does not know, and spiritually know Christ in this relation has no well-grounded hope. He may hope that he is a Christian. He may hope that his sins are forgiven, that he shall be saved. But he can have no good hope of glory. It cannot be too fully understood, or too deeply realized, that absolute despair of help and salvation in any other possible way, except by Christ in us, is an unalterable condition of our knowing and embracing Christ as our hope. Many seem to have conceived of Christ as their hope, only in his outward relation, that is, as an atoning Saviour, as a risen and ascended Saviour. But the indispensable necessity of having Christ within them, ruling in their hearts, and establishing his government over their whole being, is a condition of salvation of which they have not thought. Christ cannot be truly and savingly our hope, any farther than he is received into and reigns in our souls. To hope in merely an outward Christ is to hope in vain. To hope in Christ with the true Christian hope, implies:—

(*a*.) The ripe and spiritual apprehension of our hopeless condition without him. It implies such an apprehension of our sins and governmental relations, as to annihilate all hope of salvation upon legal grounds.

(*b.*) Such a perception of our spiritual bondage to sin, as to annihilate all hope of salvation without his constant influence and strength to keep us from sin.

(*c.*) Such a knowledge of our circumstances of temptation, as to empty us of all expectation of fighting our own battles, or of, in the least degree, making headway against our spiritual foes, in our own wisdom and strength.

(*d.*) A complete annihilation of all hope from any other source.

(*e.*) The revelation of Christ to our souls as our hope by the Holy Spirit.

(*f.*) The apprehension of him as one to dwell in us, and to be received by faith to the supreme control of our souls.

(*g.*) The hearty and joyful reception of him in this relation. The dethroning of self, or the utter denial or rejection of self, and the enthroning and crowning of Christ in the inner man. When Christ is clearly seen to be the only hope of the soul, and when he is spiritually received in this relation, the soul learns habitually and constantly to lean upon him, to rest in him, and make no efforts without him.

(liv.) Christ is also our Salvation. Ex. xv. 2: "The Lord is my strength and song, and he is become my salvation, he is my God, and I will prepare him an habitation; my father's God, and I will exalt him." Ps. xxvii. 1: "The Lord is my light and salvation, whom shall I fear? the Lord is the strength of my life; of whom shall I be afraid?" Ps. xxxviii. 22: "Make haste to help me, O Lord my salvation." Ps. lxii. 7: "In God is my salvation and my glory; the rock of my strength, and my refuge, is in God." Ps. cxiv. "The Lord is my strength and song, and is become my salvation." Isa. xii. 2: "Behold, God is my salvation; I will trust, and not be afraid; for the Lord Jehovah is my strength and my song; he also is become my salvation." Isa. xlix. 6: "And he said, It is a light thing that thou shouldest be my servant, to raise up the tribes of Jacob, and to restore the preserved of Israel; I will also give thee for a light to the Gentiles, that thou mayest be my salvation unto the ends of the earth." Luke ii. 30: "For mine eyes have seen thy salvation." These and multitudes of similar passages present Christ, not only as our Saviour, but as our salvation. That is, he saves us by becoming himself our salvation. Becoming our salvation includes and implies the following things:—

(*a*.) Atonement for our sins.

(*b*.) Convincing us of and converting us from our sins.

(*c*.) Sanctifying our souls.

(*d*.) Justifying, or pardoning and accepting, or receiving us to favour.

(*e*.) Giving us eternal life and happiness.

(*f*.) The bestowment of himself upon us as the portion of our souls.

(*g*.) The everlasting union of our souls with God.

All this Christ is to us, and well he may be regarded not only as our Saviour, but as our salvation. Nothing is or can be more important, than for us to apprehend Christ in the fulness of his relations to us. Many seem to have but extremely superficial apprehensions of Christ. They seem in a great measure blind to the length, and breadth, and height, and depth of their infinite necessities. Hence they have never sought for such a remedy as is found in Christ. The great mass of Christian professors seem to conceive of the salvation of Christ, as consisting in a state of mind resulting not from a real union of the soul with Christ, but resulting merely from understanding and believing the doctrines of Christ. The doctrine of Christ, as taught in the Bible, was designed to gain for Christ a personal reception to dwell within, and to rule over us. He that truly believes the gospel, will receive Christ as he is presented in the gospel, that is, for what he is there asserted to be to his people, in all the relations he sustains to our souls, as fast as these relations are revealed to him by the Holy Spirit.

The newly converted soul knows Christ in but few relations. He needs trials and experience to develope his weakness, and to reveal to him his multiplied necessities, and thus lead him to a fuller knowledge of Christ. The new convert embraces Christ, so far as he knows him; but at first he knows but little of his need of him, except in his governmental relations. Subsequent experience is a condition of his knowing Christ in all his fulness. Nor can he be effectually taught the fulness there is in Christ, any faster than his trials develope his real necessities. If he embraces all he understands of Christ, this is the whole of present duty in respect to him; but, as trials are in his way, he will learn more of his own necessities, and must learn more of Christ, and appropriate him in new relations, or he will surely fall.

(lv.) Christ is also the Rock of our Salvation:—

Ps. xix. 14. "Let the words of my mouth, and the meditation of my heart, be acceptable in thy sight, O Lord, my strength, [margin *Rock*] and my Redeemer. xxviii. 1. Unto, thee will I cry, O Lord my rock; be not silent to me; lest if thou be silent to me, I become like them that go down into the pit. xxxi. 2. Bow down thine ear to me, deliver me speedily, be thou my strong rock, for a house of defence to save me. 3. For thou art my rock and my fortress; therefore, for thy name's sake, lead me and guide me."

It is deeply interesting and affecting to contemplate the relations in which Christ revealed himself to the Old Testament saints. He is a rock of salvation, a strong-hold or place of refuge. In this relation the soul must know him, and must take hold of him, or take shelter in him.

(lvi.) He is also a Rock cleft from which the waters of life flow. 1 Cor. x. 14. "And did all drink the same spiritual drink, for they drank of that spiritual Rock that follow- ed them, and that Rock was Christ." As such the soul must know and embrace him.

(lvii.) He is a Great Rock that is higher than we, rising amid the burning sands of our pilgrimage, under the cooling shadow of which the soul can find repose and comfort. He is like the shadow of a great rock in a weary land. To apprehend Christ in this relation, the soul needs to be brought into sharp and protracted trials, until it is faint and ready to sink in discouragement. When the struggle is too severe for longer endurance, and the soul is on the point of giving up in despair, then when Christ is revealed as a great rock standing for its defence against the heat of its trials, and throwing over it the cooling, soothing influence of his protection, it finds itself refreshed and at rest, and readily adopts the language of a numerous class of passages of scripture, and finds itself to have apprehended Christ, as inspired men apprehended and embraced him. It is truly remarkable, that in all our experiences, we can find that inspired writers have had the like; and in every trial, and in every deliverance, in every new discovery of our emptiness, and of Christ's fulness, we find the language of our hearts most fully and aptly expressed in the language of the living oracles. We readily discover, that inspired men had fallen into like trials, had Christ revealed to them in the same relations, and had similar exercises of mind; insomuch, that no language of our own can so readily express all that we think, and feel, and see.

(lviii.) He is the Rock from which the soul is satisfied with honey. Ps. lxxxi. 16. "He should have fed them also with the finest of the wheat; and with honey out of the rock should I have satisfied thee." The spiritual mind apprehends this language spiritually, as it is doubtless really intended to be understood. It knows what it is to be satisfied with honey from the Rock, Christ. The divine sweetness that often refreshes the spiritual mind, when it betakes itself to the Rock Christ, reminds it of the words of this passage of scripture.

(lix.) He is the Rock or Foundation upon which the church, as the temple of the living God, is built.

Matt. xvi. 18: "And I say also unto thee, That thou art Peter, and upon this rock I will build my church, and the gates of hell shall not prevail against it." Rom. ix. 33: "As it is written, Behold, I lay in Sion a stumbling-stone and a rock of offence; and whosoever believeth on him shall not be ashamed." 1 Peter ii. 8. "And a stone of stumbling, and a rock of offence, even to them which stumble at the word, being disobedient; whereunto also they were appointed."

He is a sure foundation. He is an eternal rock, or the rock of ages—the corner-stone of the whole spiritual edifice. But we must build for ourselves upon this rock. It is not enough to understand as a tenet, a theory, an opinion, an article of our creed, that Christ is the rock in this sense. We must see that we do not build upon the sand. Matt. vii. 26, 27: "And every one that heareth these sayings of mine, and doeth them not, shall be likened unto a foolish man, which built his house upon the sand; And the rain descended, and the floods came, and beat upon that house; and it fell; and great was the fall of it."

(lx.) He is the "Strength of our heart." He is not only our refuge and strength in our conflicts with outward temptations and trials, in the sense expressed in Psalm xlvi. 1: "God is our refuge and strength, a very present help in trouble;" but he is also the strength of our heart and our portion for ever, in the sense of Psalm lxxiii. 26: "My flesh and my heart faileth; but God is the strength of my heart, and my portion for ever." He braces up and confirms the whole inner-man in the way of holiness. What Christian has not at times found himself ready to halt, and faint by the way. Temptation seems to steal upon him like a charm. He finds his spiritual strength very low, his resolution weak, and he feels as if he should give way to the slightest temptation. He is afraid to expose himself out of his closet, or even to remain within it lest he should sin. He says with David, "I shall fall by the hand of Saul." He finds himself empty, all weakness and trembling. Were it not that the strength of his heart interposes in time, he would doubtless realize in his experience his worst fears. But who that knows Christ, has not often experienced his faithfulness under such circumstances, and felt an immortal awaking, reviving, and strength, taking possession of his whole being? What spiritual minister has not often dragged himself into the pulpit, so discouraged and faint as to be hardly able to stand, or to hold up his head? He is so weak that his spiritual knees smite one against the other. He is truly empty, and feels as if he could not open his mouth. He sees himself to be an empty vine, an empty vessel, a poor helpless, strengthless infant, lying in the dust before the Lord, unable to stand, or go, or preach, or pray, or do the least thing for Christ. But lo! at this juncture his spiritual strength is renewed. Christ the strength of his heart developes his own almightiness within him. His mouth is open. He is strong in faith, giving glory to God. He is made at once a sharp threshing instrument, to beat down the mountains of opposition to Christ and his gospel. His bow is renewed in his hand and abides in strength. His mouth is opened, and Christ fills it with arguments. Christ has girded him to the battle, and made strong the arms of his hands, with the strength of the mighty God of Jacob.

The same in substance is true of every Christian. He has his seasons of being empty, that he may feel his dependence; and anon he is girded with strength from on high, and an immortal and superhuman strength takes possession of his soul. The enemy gives way before him. In Christ he can run through a troop, and in his strength he can leap over a wall. Every difficulty gives way before him, and he is conscious that Christ has strengthened him with strength in his soul. The will seems to have the utmost decision, so that temptation gets an emphatic no! without a moment's parley.

(lxi.) It is through Christ that we may reckon ourselves dead indeed unto sin, and alive unto God. This we are exhorted and commanded to do. That is, we may and ought to account or reckon ourselves, through him, as dead unto sin and alive unto God. But what is implied in this liberty to reckon ourselves dead unto sin, and alive unto God through Jesus Christ our Lord? Why certainly:—

(*a*.) That through and in him we have all the provision we need, to keep us from sin.

(*b*.) That we may expect, and ought to expect, to live without sin.

(*c*.) That we ought to account ourselves as having nothing more to do with sin, than a dead man has with the affairs of this world.

(*d*.) That we may and ought to lay hold of Christ for this full and present death unto sin and life unto God.

(*e*.) That if we do thus reckon ourselves dead unto sin and alive unto God, in the true spiritual sense of this text, we shall find Christ unto our souls all we expect of him in this relation. If Christ cannot or will not save us from sin, upon condition of our laying hold of him, and reckoning ourselves dead unto sin, and alive unto God through him, what right had the apostle to say, "Reckon yourselves indeed dead unto sin, and alive unto God through Jesus Christ our Lord?" What! does the apostle tell us to account or reckon ourselves dead indeed unto sin, and shall ministers tell us that such reckoning or expectation is a dangerous delusion?

Now, certainly nothing less can be meant, by reckoning ourselves dead unto sin and alive unto God through Jesus Christ, than that, through Christ we should expect to live without sin. And not to expect to live without sin through Christ is unbelief. It is a rejection of Christ in this relation. Through Christ we ought to expect to live to God, as much as we expect to live at all. He that does not expect this, rejects Christ as his sanctification, and as Jesus who saves his people from their sins.

The foregoing are some of the relations which Christ sustains to us as to our salvation. I could have enlarged greatly, as you perceive, upon each of these, and easily have swelled this part of our course of study to a large volume. I have only touched upon these sixty-one relations, as specimens of the manner in which he is presented for our acceptance in the Bible, and by the Holy Spirit. Do not understand me as teaching, that we must first know Christ in all these relations, before we can be sanctified. The thing intended is that coming to know Christ in these relations is a condition, or is the indispensable means, of our steadfastness or perseverance in holiness under temptation—that, when we are tempted, from time to time nothing can secure us against a fall, but the revelation of Christ to the soul in these relations one after another, and our appropriation of him to ourselves by faith. The gospel has directly promised, in every temptation to open a way of escape, so that we shall be able to bear it. The spirit of this promise pledges to us such a revelation of Christ, as to secure our standing, if we will lay hold upon him by faith, as revealed. Our circumstances of temptation render it necessary, that at one time we should apprehend Christ in one relation, and at another time in another. For example, at one time we are tempted to despair by Satan's accusing us of sin, and suggesting that our sins are too great to be forgiven. In this case we need a revelation and an appropriation of Christ, as having been made sin for us; that is, as having atoned for our sins—as being our justification or righteousness. This will sustain the soul's confidence and preserve its peace.

At another time we are tempted to despair of ever overcoming our tendencies to sin, and to give up our sanctification as a hopeless thing. Now we need a revelation of Christ as our sanctification, &c.

At another time the soul is harassed with the view of the great subtlety and sagacity of its spiritual enemies, and greatly tempted to despair on that account. Now it needs to know Christ as its wisdom.

Again, it is tempted to discouragement on account of the great number and strength of its adversaries. On such occasions it needs Christ revealed as the Mighty God, as its strong tower, its hiding place, its munition of rocks.

Again, the soul is oppressed with a sense of the infinite holiness of God, and the infinite distance there is between us and God, on account of our sinfulness and his infinite holiness, and on account of his infinite abhorrence of sin and sinners. Now the soul needs to know Christ as its righteousness, and as a mediator between God and man.

Again, the Christian's mouth is closed with a sense of guilt, so that he cannot look up, nor speak to God of pardon and acceptance. He trembles and is confounded before God. He lies along on his face, and despairing thoughts roll a tide of agony through his soul. He is speechless, and can only groan out his self-accusations before the Lord. Now as a condition of rising above this temptation to despair, he needs a revelation of Christ as his advocate, as his high priest, as ever living to make intercession for him. This view of Christ will enable the soul to commit all to him in this relation, and maintain its peace and hold on to its steadfastness.

Again, the soul is led to tremble in view of its constant exposedness to besetments on every side, oppressed with such a sense of its own utter helplessness in the presence of its enemies, as almost to despair. Now it needs to know Christ as the Good Shepherd, who keeps a constant watch over the sheep, and carries the lambs in his bosom. He needs to know him as a watchman and a keeper.

Again, it is oppressed with a sense of its own utter emptiness, and is forced to exclaim, I know that in me, that is, in my flesh, dwelleth no good thing. It sees that it has no life, or unction, or power, or spirituality in itself. Now it needs to know Christ as the true vine, from which it may receive constant and abundant spiritual nourishment. It needs to know him as the fountain of the water of life, and in those relations that will meet its necessities in this direction. Let these suffice, as specimens to illustrate what is intended by entire or permanent sanctification being conditioned on the revelation and appropriation of Christ in all the fulness of his official relations.

It is not intended, as has been said, that Christ must previously be known in all these relations before a soul can be sanctified at all; but that, when tried from time to time, a new revelation of Christ to the soul, corresponding to the temptation, or as the help of the soul in such circumstances, is a condition of its remaining steadfast. This gracious aid or revelation is abundantly promised in the Bible, and will be made in time, so that by laying hold on Christ in the present revealed relation, the soul may be preserved blameless, though the furnace of temptation be heated seven times hotter than it is wont to be.

In my estimation, the church, as a body—I mean the nominal church—have entirely mistaken the nature and means or conditions of sanctification. They have not regarded it as consisting in a state of entire consecration, nor understood that continual entire consecration was entire sanctification. They have regarded sanctification as consisting in the annihilation of the constitutional propensities, instead of the controlling of them. They have erred equally in regard to the means or conditions of entire sanctification. They seem to have regarded sanctification as brought about by a physical cleansing in which man was passive; or to have gone over to the opposite extreme, and regarded sanctification as consisting in the formation of habits of obedience. The old school have seemed to be waiting for a physical sanctification, in which they are to be, in a great measure, passive, and which they have not expected to take place in this life. Holding, as they do, that the constitution of both soul and body is defiled or sinful in every power and faculty, they of course cannot hold to entire sanctification in this life. If the constitutional appetites, passions, and propensities are in fact, as they hold, sinful in themselves, why then the question is settled, that entire sanctification cannot take place in this world, nor in the next, except as the constitution is radically changed, and that of course by the creative power of God. The new school, rejecting the doctrine of constitutional moral depravity, and physical regeneration and sanctification, and losing sight of Christ as our sanctification, have fallen into a self-righteous view of sanctification, and have held that sanctification is effected by works, or by forming holy habits, &c. Both the old and the new school have fallen into egregious errors upon this fundamentally important subject.

The truth is, beyond all question, that sanctification is by faith as opposed to works. That is, faith receives Christ in all his offices, and in all the fulness of his relations to the soul; and Christ, when received, works in the soul to will and to do of all his good pleasure, not by a physical, but by a moral or persuasive working. Observe, he influences the will. This must be by a moral influence, if its actings are intelligent and free, as they must be to be holy. That is, if he influences the will to obey God, it must be by a divine moral suasion. The soul never in any instance obeys in a spiritual and true sense, except it be thus influenced by the indwelling Spirit of Christ. But whenever Christ is apprehended and received in any relation, in that relation he is full and perfect; so that we are complete in him. For it hath pleased the Father that in him should all fulness dwell; and that we might all receive of his fulness until we have grown up into him in all things, "Until we all come, in the unity of the faith and of the knowledge of the Son of God, unto a perfect man, unto the measure of the stature of the fulness of Christ."

www.ingramcontent.com/pod-product-compliance
Lightning Source LLC
Chambersburg PA
CBHW062209080426
42734CB00010B/1857